William Chambers Morrow

Blood-Money

William Chambers Morrow

Blood-Money

ISBN/EAN: 9783743325456

Manufactured in Europe, USA, Canada, Australia, Japa

Cover: Foto ©ninafisch / pixelio.de

Manufactured and distributed by brebook publishing software (www.brebook.com)

William Chambers Morrow

Blood-Money

BY

WILLIAM C. MORROW.

SAN FRANCISCO:
F. J. WALKER & CO.
1882.

Copyright, 1882,
By F. J. WALKER & Co.

BACON & COMPANY, PRINTERS.

CONTENTS.

CHAPTER I.
A Mysterious Letter . . . . PAGE 7

CHAPTER II.
The Lone Tree Treasure 13

CHAPTER III.
The Terror of Despair 22

CHAPTER IV.
The Search Commenced 29

CHAPTER V.
A Midnight Revelation 42

CHAPTER VI.
A Strange Visitor 57

CHAPTER VII.
Nellie's New Friends 70

CHAPTER VIII.
Blackmail 79

CHAPTER IX.
Covill's Announcement 89

CHAPTER X.
New Developments 96

CHAPTER XI.
A Tradegy on the Plains 105

CHAPTER XII.
The "Sand-Lappers." 115

CHAPTER XIII.
A Duel with Death 131

CHAPTER XIV.
A Rupture 145

CHAPTER XV.
An Apparition 154

CHAPTER XVI.
Returned to Life 160

CHAPTER XVII.
The Warning 166

CHAPTER XVIII.
The Eleventh of May 179

CHAPTER XIX.

THE BAPTISM OF BLOOD 188

CHAPTER XX.

A DISCOVERY 196

CHAPTER XXI.

A VERY LONG JOURNEY 205

CHAPTER XXII.

THE END OF THE SEARCH 214

CHAPTER XXIII.

A TREASURE LOST AND A TREASURE FOUND . . . 229

BLOOD-MONEY.

CHAPTER I.

A MYSTERIOUS LETTER.

FOUR or five years ago there lived in the heart of the San Joaquin Valley, California, a young man about twenty-five years of age. His only companion was his grandmother—an aged and feeble woman, in whose palsied hands and trembling voice there were traces of other wearing agencies than the accumulation of years and natural infirmities. Grief, which is more wasting than time, had set its mark upon her face. Nevertheless, in the last years of her life a great comfort had come to her, in the shape of her grandson, whom she loved and clung to and idolized with all a mother's love. Her feeble life was bound up in him. She took a great interest in everything that concerned him; and although the time had long ago passed when his strong young nature asserted undisputed supremacy over hers, and although she no longer directed and controlled the affairs that were common to them, yet she assisted and encouraged him all in her power, and rendered him material aid.

Consequently she was as deeply concerned as he, when he returned one day from the village with a letter directed to him. He had never received a letter before, and the sensation was novel. So little did he know of the great world that lay beyond the horizon of the level plains, and so bewildered was he at holding in his hand a letter addressed to his own name, that he hurried with it unopened to his grandmother. The old lady, curious as he, and wondering at the arrival of a letter, opened it, and they read it together. It was written in red ink. The writing was in a scrawling, irregular hand. There was no signature of any kind, no date, and no introduction. The orthography was as bad as the handwriting. Shorn of these defects, the letter read as follows:

"There is a tree in Tulare County called Lone Tree. Everybody knows where it is. It is a large, old oak, and stands six or seven miles north of Tulare Lake. You will have no trouble in finding it, as all the people in that part of the country know where it is. Hence it is unnecessary for me to describe it. Eighteen years ago a cross was cut into the side of the tree facing the east, and exactly five feet from the ground. When you have found the tree, measure five feet from the base eastward by the compass, then four feet northward. Then dig. You will find an iron pot, and inside the pot twenty-two thousand dollars in gold coin. Take the money, and use it as you please, for it is yours. Above all things, as you value your life, say nothing to anybody about it. If you obey this injunction, you will never be disturbed."

The astonishment of the two who read this letter, deciphering it with much trouble, cannot be described. They stared at each other in amazement, unable for some time to say anything. Twenty-two thousand dollars! What did it mean?

"Grandmother," said the young man at last, tearing the dream painfully from his heart, "this is certainly a foolish joke."

She did not seem to hear him, nor even to see him; for although she looked at him, it could be plainly seen that her mind was far away with the dim memories of the past. An old look of pain, which the young man had often seen, came into her face, and settled itself there firmly.

"John," she finally said, "I don't believe it's a joke. It says twenty-two thousand dollars, doesn't it?"

"Yes, grandmother."

"That money is yours, John. You ought to have had it long ago."

The young man gazed at her, dumb with astonishment.

"It has been yours by right, John, for eighteen years—ever since that day, eighteen years ago, when they brought my son to me—your father, John—dead—murdered for his money."

"I remember it," the young man softly replied, while his mind was busy with the problem that the old woman had already solved.

"Your father was a rich man then, John, and that was the cause of his death. Eighteen years ago he bought a great stock-range, covering nearly all the eastern part of this county, and intended to raise cattle on a large scale. He had thousands of cattle; and besides, he had ten thousand dollars to his credit in San Francisco. He sold all his stock and his old range, and was on his way home from San Francisco with the money when he was murdered. The money was a good load, but he had a strong horse. He wasn't afraid of anything living, John. You are just the image of him, and when you are older you will be as brave as he was. I don't say that you ain't brave now; but your father wasn't timid and bashful, although he was when he was a young man."

In the excitement natural to her under the circumstances, she lost the sequence of her thoughts, and then checked her rambling remarks. After a moment of silence the idea she had in her mind recurred to her, and looking straight at her grandson, she asked:

"Do you know how much money he had with him when he was murdered, John?"

"I don't remember, grandmother."

"Well, that letter tells you."

"Twenty-two thousand dollars?"

"Yes."

"Well, grandmother," said John, half divining the old woman's meaning, but afraid of committing an error, "what has the twenty-two thousand dollars buried under Lone Tree to do with my father's money?"

"It's the same money, John."

The young man held his breath, as he realized the strong probability that the money under Lone Tree was conscience-money; and that the murderer, after eighteen years, had thus voluntarily surrendered to the rightful owner the money that came by blood. He gasped for breath at the prospect of a wonderful fortune so suddenly brought within his grasp —a fortune greater than that ever pictured in his day-dreams, dazzling in its splendor, overpowering in its magnificence, and lifting him far above the surroundings of his humble lot. It is not surprising that his heart throbbed wildly, and that visions of enchantment appeared to his excited imagination. Nor is it a matter of surprise that the sudden and dangerous ecstasy into which he was thrown by the prospect of these splendid riches gave little opportunity for a quickening of sorrow, as the terrible tragedy that rendered him an orphan was thus almost re-enacted before his eyes. The old woman sat and brooded in silence over what was still fresh in her failing memory; but a glance at the flushed face and sparkling eyes of her grandson brought her back to the present, and she was joyous for his sake.

"It will make you a great, rich man, John; and I know you will always be a good man."

In order to have a clear conception of the extraordinary vicissitudes through which John Graham passed after the receipt of the mysterious letter, it will be necessary to have some knowledge of his character and personal appearance. He was of the average size of men, and had a fair complexion and blue eyes. Hard work in the pure open air of the plains had toughened his muscles, and there was no young man of his acquaintance who was his rival in feats of strength. By nature he was ambitious; but so unselfish and patient was he that no one knew of his dreams. He never complained, and his energy never abated. Although bashful and apparently timid, he was by nature utterly dauntless. A woman could frighten him, but a man could not. Underlying all other traits, and as yet unknown even to him, was a stern stubbornness, that was capable of desperate urgings in an extremity, and that would strangle and murder if driven to the wall. This hidden ferocity of nature was at present subservient to a natural goodness that trying circumstances had not yet chilled; and in any event, he possessed that natural caution which necessarily comes with wholesome courage.

He had a fair education: his grandmother, who herself had had tender rearing, taking great pride in his quick susceptibility of knowledge under her careful but not thoroughly efficient training.

He was not a man given up to a ready acceptance of every plausible thing that presented itself; but the magnitude of the import of the anonymous letter overcame his cooler judgment, and suffused his imagination with the wildest dreams.

CHAPTER II.

THE LONE TREE TREASURE.

WITHOUT delay John Graham set out to discover the treasure buried at the foot of Lone Tree. It may be here remarked, that there seems to be in California a fashion of naming every isolated tree " Lone Tree." The writer of the anonymous letter was perhaps not fully aware of that fact. He should have reflected, especially, that the broad stretch of oak timber that surrounds the quaint old town of Visalia is a great rarity on the plains, this being the only oak belt in the San Joaquin Valley; and that the scattering outposts of this army of oaks surrounding Visalia, and repelling the furious assaults of sand-storms sweeping down from Merced, are objects of considerable attention. Besides, other trees stand at intervals about the borders of the lake. The willows that abound in Mussel Slough—a section of magnificent country lying north of the lake, and which takes its name from a slough that makes out from the lake—the willows that there abound attract far less attention than do the occasional solitary oaks that still remain as relics of a forest that passed away centuries ago. Now, the writer of the mysterious letter would have known, had he been better acquainted with the country thereabout, that there are now several stately old forest kings there, each bearing the name of Lone Tree. As the inhabitants of a country settle the decrees of fate, so far as geographical nomenclature is concerned, it would hardly be fair to find fault with the condition of things as they now exist; and it has come to be so that, in the minds of local geographers, there is much doubt as to which Lone Tree is the only original Lone Tree of early local history. As the new order of things has come about under the natural operation of the laws of progress and civilization, it would be hardly just to attach blame to anybody, or to assume that the unknown writer of the letter might have kept himself informed in contemporaneous history, so that the identity of the only original Lone Tree should not be swallowed up by the tendencies of advancement toward multiplication. Certain it is, that the existence of more than one Lone Tree proved a serious stumbling-block to John Graham. That the writer of the letter did not know that Lone Tree had been multiplied indefinitely was evidence of the fact that he had not visited that section of country for many years.

Indeed, as Graham was comparatively a stranger in that particular section of country, he had to learn, by hard experience, that Lone Tree, for all he knew, might exist at intervals indefinitely all over the world.

He arrived in the Mussel Slough country the day following the receipt of the letter, and inquired for Lone Tree. He had ridden his horse, and had brought with him some food, a pick, a shovel, and his grandmother's blessing. He did not search far before he found a man who told him where Lone Tree was.

After a short hunt the young man found it. His heart beat high as he secured his horse to a neighboring willow and approached Lone Tree. Would he find the treasure? or would his bright dreams be routed and scattered to the winds? To his excited vision the lonely tree had an awful look. The branches waived ominously, as though shaken by a horde of ghosts suddenly put to flight; and the gnarled and twisted and deformed branches appeared to be, one a man helplessly struggling for his life, the other a murderer wielding a cruel bludgeon, and dashing out the brains of the victim. The silence of the midday, when not even a bird twittered in the willows, was appalling.

But the young man was sturdy and stout of heart, and he thrust these unwholesome visions aside, and pushed on to the task—a simple one—that lay before him.

He searched that side of the trunk turned to the east for a cross, but found none. He was not discouraged by this, for the reason that the cross might have been obliterated by time. Certainly, however, he could not find any trace of a cross.

Nothing daunted, he carefully measured off the ground, under the explicit directions of the letter, and commenced to dig, having first assured himself that no one was watching him. While hardly permitting himself to believe it, he could not, if he would, have abandoned the hope that twenty-two thousand dollars in bright gold lay just under his feet, and almost within his grasp.

He rapidly penetrated the yielding, sandy soil found almost exclusively in that section. His shovel piled the dirt on either side. He was digging a hole about four feet square, to allow for inaccuracies of measurement. Time flew swiftly, and the hole deepened visibly under the steady, almost furious, work of his strong arms.

Presently a gloomy idea, that had been silently taking possession of his mind without his knowledge, gained sudden mastery over him, and paralyzed his arm. The surface of the ground was level with his shoulders, and yet he had discovered no trace of a pot. A realization of the futility of further digging burst upon him with irresistible force. The bitterness of that blow entered his heart like iron, and hurt like a knife in the flesh. His first impulse was despair, and the next furious anger.

"It was all a lie!" he muttered, with terrible anger. "It was a cruel lie, to make a fool of me. If I knew who the scoundrel is, I'd—"

There is no doubt about it. He would then and there have carried out any threat, expressed or thought, stopping at nothing short of murder.

"If I had only myself to think of," he muttered, somewhat in a philosophical vein, "I wouldn't care so much; but I was thinking of Nellie, and of how fond she is of fine things, and of how handsome she would look, and of how we could travel after we marry, and all that. I say it's a downright shame—a damnable shame!"

That was the first expression of such a nature that had ever passed his lips.

After the first heat of anger had cooled, he discovered that he was very tired. The afternoon was wearing away, and in two hours the sun would set. The young man calmed himself sufficiently to reflect on the plausibility of the theory advanced by his grandmother, and on the possibility of error in the directions given by the letter, or on his own part, in various ways. He was too much exhausted to work more that day; and mounting his horse, he rode away to find shelter for the night, his own home being many miles distant. As he moved away he again looked for the mysterious rustling of the leaves, and the hideously grotesque shapes that the branches of Lone Tree took at first; but, strange to say, he saw only a very ugly, ill-shaped tree—verily a lone tree in point of an ugliness so intense as to be almost picturesque.

That night at the house of his host he brought up the subject of Lone Tree, and learned, to his astonishment, that there were several trees of that name in that part of the country. It discouraged him in the sense that possibly he might have to dig for the treasure under every Lone Tree in the country; but it encouraged him to think that his failure to succeed with the first was not evidence that he would experience similar ill fortune with all the others.

The task that now confronted him was to ascertain, if possible, the tree that was called Lone Tree eighteen years ago; there evidently having been but one such tree at that time, as otherwise the letter would have mentioned it, and left no room for doubt.

It is a safe assertion that John Graham slept little that

night; and that when he did sleep, unpleasant dreams, wherein blood and gold were mingled—as nearly always they are—came to disturb his rest. It is unnecessary to follow him in his energetic but guarded efforts to find the Lone Tree under which the treasure was possibly buried. After a search of three days he did find the tree, and on that side of it facing the rising sun was a dimly outlined Swiss cross, all awry with age, and distinguishable only by one who was earnestly looking for it.

The young man's heart bounded with a furious delight as he traced the cross in the bark. So eager and excited was he, that he failed to notice a man standing a few rods away and eyeing him curiously.

Graham, with an accuracy that may be called, with some men, an intuition, measured the ground with his eye. Weeds and grass grew tall and rank in the immediate vicinity of Lone Tree, and the surrounding ground was under cultivation. The man who was watching Graham with so much interest was the owner of the field in which Lone Tree stood. It cannot be said that this man had a pleasant face; but that might be because he was ugly almost to a sinful extent. He had a pointed chin, a small mouth, a thin hooked nose, pale blue eyes, that were very piercing, a low forehead, and his face was covered with a thin set of sandy whiskers. This man did not inspire confidence with certain other men. He also, as well as Graham, is a person of some use to this simple story.

When Graham had located, with perfect accuracy, the spot indicated in the letter, he saw a thing that made his heart stand still. It was evident that within the last few months the dirt there had been disturbed. This revelation, bringing with it the idea that possibly the treasure had already been taken away, caused Graham to stagger backward. As he did so, his foot caught in the rim of an iron pot; and Graham, tripped by the pot and stunned by the revelation, fell heavily to the ground.

He immediately roused himself and glared about him. None who have never felt it can realize the weight of the shock that comes when the fondest hope in life is suddenly and violently strangled.

While Graham was thus sitting, a thin, wiry, nasal voice, entering the ear like a corkscrew, and burrowing in the brain like an earwig, called:

"Hey!"

This hail was insulting in fact and impudent in essence. Graham possessed natural dignity of character, and intuitively resented any unwarranted familiarity. He rose to his feet, and glared around to discover the source of the voice, and found it. He regarded the intruder with silent scorn; but at the same time he felt himself in an undignified position, and his cheeks flushed with shame that he should be discovered.

"What are yer doin' ther?" asked the intruder, who for some reason of his own did not advance nearer the treasure hunter. Graham maintained a stolid and combative silence.

"I was a-goin' to say," continued the older man, "that if ye're a-lookin' fer that treasure, some other feller's got ahead o' yer."

"What do you mean?" asked Graham, considerably interested, but none the less on his guard.

"Wall, yer'll have to git up soon to git ahead of a priest."

"A priest!"

"Yes; a priest. He got the treasure. Say, how 'd yer know ther was any treasure ther? I've been here two year, an' I never knowed it."

Graham vouchsafed no reply.

"Might I ask wher yer live?"

Graham said nothing. The older man, desiring for his own gratification to learn more of Graham's connection with the mystery surrounding the affair, said:

"My little boy Frank seen him dig the treasure up and take it away. I'll call Frank, an' he kin tell yer more about it. Hey! Frankie! Frankie! Come here!"

A dirty little urchin came running to the spot, from a slough where he had been amusing himself by trying to train his mother's chickens to swim in the pool.

"Frankie, tell this man all about the priest; an' how he dug up the treasure an' took it away."

The boy, not at all abashed by the presence of a stranger, told the following story, in a voice and manner that would have rendered unnecessary any uneasiness on his father's part as to the boy's paternal origin:

"Waal, me 'n Jim—that's my little brother, you know—was a-throwin' rocks at some birds in them willers there, an' putty soon Jim, he says, 'What's that?' an' I says, 'What's what?' an' he says, ''Tain't what; it's a buggy'; an' then I looks, an' I see a buggy, an' it was a-turnin' out'n that road over there, an' was a-coming right after us, an' I says to Jim, 'Le's hide,' an' we got down on our bellies under the willers, an' we could see all the time. Then the buggy it driv up to Lone Tree an' stopped, an' a man got out, all dressed in black, an' no whiskers, an' measured on the groun', an' then commenced—"

"That was a priest," interrupted his father.

"Yes, a pries', all buttoned up to the chin, an' he worked and digged like fury, an' then putty soon he fetched up a iron pot, an' knocked off the lid, an' poured a *great big* pile o' money in a sack, an' then he put it in the buggy an' driv off."

Frank was entirely out of breath when he had finished this minute and satisfactory recital, and his father plied Graham with judicious questions, but received no satisfaction. The young man thanked him for his trouble; and mounting his horse, rode away, weary in body, crushed, broken, and humiliated in spirit, and nursing unconsciously in his heart the germs of a deep, desperate, and bitter determination. This, although he had not yet met it face to face, was that he would clear up the mystery of the stolen treasure, and avenge the murder of his father. Perhaps if he could have known in time that this determination was insidiously establishing itself in his heart, he would have thrust it aside, forgotten the dream of wealth, returned to the old shadowy memory of his father's murder, and settled down to the life to which he had been accustomed since his birth. But the poison had been drunk too deeply. It mastered him. He would in turn master all that it led him to. Such was his nature; and one would say that he was not quick-witted enough for the task that confronted him, though he lacked not courage and perseverance.

CHAPTER III.

THE TERROR OF DESPAIR.

IT was with a heavy heart, almost bursting with the weight of its disappointment and humiliation, that John Graham approached the small house that had been his home for a few years past. The entire face of nature and the whole expression of home were changed to him now. A great load had fastened itself upon him, clinging to him like the Old Man of the Sea, and beating him and urging him onward to the goal that lay before him. It might not have been so had his nature been different. He possessed a depth of character, a strength of will, a pertinacity of purpose, a stubbornness of adamantine resistance at the appearance of opposition, that he had not yet even dreamed of, and that he did not realize, and that would in good time change the bashful, quiet, country boy into a man, with a will to follow a terrible purpose to its accomplishment; though it may lead him through fire, and though it may bring him to a footing up of that final account which strikes the balance of life. He was slow of purpose and tardy of execution; but once in motion, the momentum would carry him through without faltering, without a regret.

He cared no longer for the bright spring flowers that covered the plains, a gorgeous carpet from the Maker's own hand. He heeded not the squirrels that, frightened at his approach, darted into their holes in the ground. The grand Sierra, looming up before him as he slowly rode along, and which in his fancy he had often imagined to be gigantic monarchs, hoary with time, standing guard over the boundless plains and the people thereof, inspired neither awe nor reverence now. His youthful spirit was quenched, and in a single day he had become a man. The old dreams that long had brightened his youth passed out, and were scattered by the winds that bore silent tidings from Yosemite to Tejon; and grim shadows that crawled out from the cañons in the mountains, and homeless ghosts that shivered in the breeze that swept over the lake, took up their abiding place in the deserted home of the dreams.

The old home, with its bright green poplars, and its little patch of geraniums and verbenas in front, gave rise, as it came upon his view, to no sense of inviting rest. It seemed poor and drear and comfortless. And when he saw the aged grandmother standing in the door, and with her palsied hand shading her eyes from the glaring light that suffused the earth, his heart sank to its lowest depths, and for the first time in his life he wished he were dead. When the failing eyes of the old woman recognized the boy she loved more than her life, she waved her handkerchief, as she had often done before; but the accustomed greeting in return did not come. She boded evil, and her withered hand dropped listless to her side.

John looked to neither right nor left, but rode straight to the barn, removed the saddle and bridle with his accustomed care, pitched the hungry animal its modicum of hay, and with a heavy step turned toward the house. The old woman had left the front door and gone to the rear, and there she awaited her grandson. It had been her custom always to follow him to the barn, but on this day a dread kept her back. She had always been a weak and timid woman, but never until this day had she feared her grandson.

"John!" she said in a timid, quailing voice of welcome, as the young man approached the door wherein she stood.

"Grandmother!" he replied; but not with the tenderness and light-hearted freedom of old. A harsher and deeper and sterner voice spoke to her now, and frightened her. He mounted the single step that led up to the threshold, and she instinctively stood aside to let him pass. It was then that the great change in her manner impressed itself upon him, and he looked at her a moment in surprise.

"Grandmother," he said, "aren't you glad to see me? I failed, but don't blame me for that." There was a faint tinge of reproach in his tone, and it cut her to the quick.

"I don't blame you, my darling boy," and the tears trickled rapidly down her wrinkled cheeks. She would have given the world to throw her arms around his neck, and kiss his hot face and his burning lips.

"Then, grandmother, why do you act so strangely? You used to be glad to see me when I came, and now you stand back and look at me as if I were a wild animal."

The poor old woman did not know his nature, and was

ignorant of the change that had taken place within him. She could not know that the grandson she loved had died, and was buried in the shadow of Lone Tree; and that, masquerading as her boy, there came to her house that day a man whom well she might fear, and whose manner invited no caresses. She could say nothing, and could only stand and weep before him.

"Have you, too, grandmother," he said, the light brightening in his eyes, the color deepening in his cheeks, and the hardness of his voice increasing—"have you, too, turned your back upon me? Must I bear this blow, in addition to the murder of my father and the theft of his money?"

All the hidden ferocity of his nature came to the surface, and the poison boiled in his blood and made a madman of him.

"If so," he said, "let it be. And will Nellie, too, learn to hate me? Do you think, grandmother, that I will submit and cringe like a coward to all these things? No, grandmother! I'll take up the fight against this man who murdered my father, stole his money, and destroyed the happiness of my home. I'll hunt him to death. Do you hear that, grandmother? I'll hunt him to his hole, and cut out his heart with my own hands; and I'll send his cowardly soul to hell, and pray God to damn him forever, and to curse his children with disease and insanity. Do you hear that, grandmother?"

He turned to leave, and through the wild madness that dimmed his sight and caused the room to swim before his eyes, he saw, standing on the threshold, the trembling and terror-stricken form of a girl. She stood like the Angel with the flaming sword. He staggered backward before this apparition, and exclaimed:

"Nellie, I have been cheated and fooled. The whole world is against me. My own grandmother hates me. You will do as the rest have done. Stand aside, and don't touch me!"

"John!"

"Stand aside, I tell you! I know what you are going to say. I tell you it wasn't my fault. Stand aside, Nellie! Don't look at me that way! Hell is in me now, and if you look at me so, you may drive me to murder you with the rest of them."

The undaunted girl, moving not an inch, and recovering the nerve natural to her under trying circumstances, stood in his way like the Angel at the Gate, as he attempted to pass out, and continued to gaze steadfastly upon him. Burning with rage and desperation, knowing not what he did, but blind with the fury of the maddened devils within him, he rushed a short distance toward her; then a strange look suddenly came in his eyes; he stopped, threw up his hands as does a drowning man, clutched wildly at the air, ground his teeth, toppled, and fell heavily to the floor.

He lay still as death. The two women looked at each other with terror in their faces. The old grandmother tottered toward him, and fell on the floor at his side, and covered his cold face with kisses, and wept, and moaned piteously:

"My poor boy! my poor boy! I didn't mean to do it!"

The younger woman knelt on the other side, and tenderly

caressed the inert hands. Then she raised the grandmother and seated her on a chair; and then brought a pillow and placed it under John's head; and then chafed his hands, and begged him to speak to her, while the tears streamed down her pallid cheeks and a terrible fear seized her heart. The old woman could only rock and moan.

In a short time the unconscious man sighed heavily; and then sighed again, and moved uneasily on the floor. As if by a violent effort of almost unconscious will, he mastered his helplessness, opened his eyes, and looked hurriedly around, as though fearful of seeing some unearthly specter. He laboriously assumed a sitting posture, and put his hands to his head. Then he looked at the girl and smiled faintly, and looked at his grandmother with a wondering air, and extended his hand to the girl, who grasped his.

"Good morning, Nellie," he said, with the greatest kindness and tenderness.

"Good morning, John."

"Have I been asleep, Nellie?"

"Yes."

"I must have slept long, for I have a frightful headache."

"You'll be better directly, John."

"But I feel so strange and unnatural. I think I cannot be well. Grandmother, what is the matter? Have you been crying?"

All the old gentleness and tenderness, so sweet to the ears of the old woman now, were in his voice and his manner. He glanced from his grandmother to Nellie, and did not seem to understand something. A look of perplexity came into his face.

"Is there anything the matter, Nellie—grandmother?"

"Nothing whatever, John," replied the girl, her lips slightly quivering.

John attempted to rise to his feet, but he staggered, and Nellie took his arm.

"This is very strange," he said, as he regained his feet and clung to Nellie's arms to steady himself. "I never felt so before. Everything seems to be turning around. My head is so heavy! Nellie, dear, please help me to the next room, and I will lie down. I feel very drowsy, somehow; and it's an unusual thing for me to be sleepy in the daytime. I think that if I sleep a while I shall be better."

The old woman hurried ahead and arranged the bed for him; and leaning heavily on Nellie, he went into the room, and fell upon the bed. Nellie removed his shoes, and he thanked her tenderly. She sat by the bed, and took his hand in hers. With a smile full of love and gentleness—and, in fact, he was meeker and more patient than ever before—he closed his eyes, and in a moment was sound asleep.

CHAPTER IV.

THE SEARCH COMMENCED.

THEY watched him as he slumbered. After the first heavy stupor, resulting from nervous prostration, had passed away, he became restless, and muttered unintelligible words, and tossed from side to side. When four or five hours had passed, he awoke. They spoke to him kindly, and watched his expression anxiously. He was now refreshed, and in full possession of all his faculties. It was soon evident that he remembered nothing from the time when he led his horse to the barn, and they did not mention his wild fury before the faint overcame him. A hard look was in his face—the reflex of a determination that had insidiously shaped itself into form—a purpose based on an iron will and an inflexible stubbornness—dark, deep, and irrevocable. Nellie saw it and understood it; for she knew of the letter and the unsuccessful search for the buried treasure; but she was happy to see that he felt no resentment toward her and his grandmother, and that his determination in nowise changed his feeling for them. His conduct after his arrival was the result of madness, brought on by despair.

Nellie Foster was in very few respects suited to become the wife of John Graham. There were marked differences in these two young people, who loved each other fondly, and who were to be married within the year. She was pretty, vivacious, witty, and quick to learn; but she had no depth of character, no latent trait but courage. Her nature was apparent to all: vain of her comeliness, fond of finery, and ambitious to a dangerous extent. She believed that she was fitted to adorn a higher circle of society, and no doubt she was. By nature she was qualified to become a dashing woman of the world, courting admiration, conquering hearts, and trampling under foot everything that opposed her wishes. She had never had opportunity to shine in the world. She, like Graham, was an orphan; and doubtless it was their common desolation that first drew them together. She lived with an uncle, who, though a kind-hearted and indulgent man, was compelled, by reason of straightened circumstances, to deny his winsome niece a hundred things that he knew would make her heart glad. She was full of energy, a nervous, restless, and indefatigable worker, and was really the controlling, not to say domineering, spirit in her uncle's house. Her aunt was a meek, submissive woman, and Nellie had a way of ruling her and all the others that was pretty and amusing. None were so bright and cheerful as Nellie. She sang and laughed and talked the whole day long. Many were the sturdy, industrious young fellows who had thrown themselves at her shapely feet and pleaded for her hand; but she had laughed at them all, and sent them away wondering whether she was a woman or a devil.

When John Graham, scarcely more than a year prior to the opening of this story, presented himself, she saw in his square chin and calm blue eye a depth of strength and manhood she never had seen before. With the quick, searching, and accurate divination that belonged to her, she saw in him a placid, quiet, grave, and patient man, willing to give his life for a friend; unselfish and generous to a rare extent; deep and silent; but for all that—which was enough to make her look up to him and respect him—there was something else: this man was a slumbering lion, slow to be aroused, but terrible, desperate, unflinching, when brought to bay or driven to an extremity. All this she dimly saw, but unconsciously. For the other, she respected him; for this, she feared him. Such a man, before all others, she would crown the king of her heart and life.

But how was it with him? Should such a woman be his wife? Could a coquette, shrewd, scheming, and vain, fill the measure of his happiness? Should his wife be a selfish woman? Was Nellie selfish? In all the wide, wide world, is there ever vanity without selfishness? Is there ever vanity without heartlessness? without a lack of charity? without a lack of dignity of soul and purity of heart?

A shadowy phantom had risen up unbidden between these two loving people—not a phantom that Graham saw, but one that appeared to the keener sight of the girl. As yet it had the innocent guise of regret, and the implanting of ambitious and disturbing longings. Living near Graham, it was her custom to visit the grandmother every day while John was in the field at work, and she thus at once learned of the mysterious letter, and afterward of the failure to find the treasure. During the time that John was absent, she indulged in dreams of oriental magnificence, wherein she was the center of all attraction. When these dreams were dashed to the ground and broken into fragments, the blow was crushing and stupefying. It was not surprising, then, that she offered no objection when John quietly remarked after his sleep:

"Grandmother, I have decided to hunt for a solution of this mystery. If the money is mine, I would be a coward to sit down and resign myself to being robbed. It is late to think now of revenging my father's murder, but in accomplishing one end the other will be served also."

Nellie's eyes sparkled with pleasure, and she smiled encouragingly on John. The elder woman said nothing, but it could be seen that the old, familiar look of pain was in her face; whether from the memory of things that were past, or on account of John's determination, he did not know. It troubled him, and he asked:

"Grandmother, do you oppose the idea?"

"Well, John," she said, after a pause, "you are doing pretty well now, and you know they are talking of some trouble about the land. Ain't you afraid that we can't make enough to live on, and that we might lose the place, if you quit earning anything? Besides, who'll harvest the crop?"

John was silent a long time. Then he said:

"You shall never be in want, grandmother. I will not leave you entirely, but shall be absent only at times; and when I am away you will stay with grandmother, will you not, Nellie?"

"Yes," exclaimed Nellie cheerily, and nodding encouragingly to the poor old lady.

"And as for the crop," continued John, "I will harvest it; and I hope we shall make enough to buy a home if they turn us out of this place."

"Ain't you afraid, John," persisted the grandmother, with some timidity, "that something may happen to you?"

"I will not put my life in danger, grandmother. On the contrary, I would have every incentive to take the best care of myself," and he looked significantly at Nellie, who dropped her glance to the floor. "Besides," he continued, "I am not sure that I shall be warranted in undertaking this matter. I am not a detective, and am not able to employ one. But we shall first see what we can find out now. Grandmother, think carefully over all the circumstances surrounding my father's death. You think there can be no doubt that robbery was the sole object of the murder?"

"It couldn't have been anything else, John. Your father was one of the best men I ever saw, and he didn't have an enemy in the world."

"But don't you think it is possible that the money was taken in order to divert attention from the true cause of the murder? It is a very extraordinary thing for a murderer to have enough conscience to restore money which was obtained through murder."

"I know it, John; but there couldn't have been any other cause."

"My mother died soon afterward, didn't she?"

"Yes; the shock killed her."

"Another account to settle with them," muttered John to himself, with something of the fireceness he had exhibited in the morning. "Isn't it possible, grandmother, that some envious man killed him through jealousy, on account of his prosperity?"

"Why should he, John? Your father was such a good man, and helped so many people in distress, and was so liberal with his money, and did so much good everywhere, that nobody could be envious of him. He wasn't a proud man, and didn't consider himself better than anybody else."

"Did he ever have a difficulty with anybody before he came to California?"

"Not to amount to anything. Of course he wouldn't allow people to impose on him; and he was a fearless man, and sometimes he had to be severe. But I don't think anybody could have laid it up against him."

"Did suspicion point to anybody at the time?"

"No. Of course we had nobody to hunt the matter up; but there were some officers who did all they could to get at the bottom of it, and the neighbors took a hand in it; but no trace was ever found, of either the murderer or the money."

"Did the officers track my father from San Francisco?"

"Yes; they trailed him to within a few miles of the spot where he was murdered, which was about five miles from home."

"No one traveled with him?"

"No one."

"Nor behind him a few miles?"

"No: not after he crossed the Coast Range and came down into the valley."

"Did any of the officers express any idea on the subject?"

"Well, they held a consultation about a week after the murder—your mother was lying dangerously sick then in the house—and they came to the conclusion that men in San Francisco knew of his having money, and came on ahead and waylaid him."

The young man reflected a while, and then said:

"That was plausible then, but it isn't now. If it had been men from San Francisco, they would have taken the money with them, and would not have buried it under Lone Tree. Of course the officers didn't know then that the money was buried there, and hence their theory was plausible. Grandmother, think carefully over what I am going to ask you: Did anybody in the neighborhood leave about that time, or shortly afterward?"

She reflected a long time, and then shook her head.

"No, John," she said; "nobody left."

"Are you perfectly sure, grandmother?"

"Perfectly sure."

"Remember that you were distracted with grief, and that a great many things might have happened that you wouldn't notice."

"That's true; but there were so few people living here then, that I should have known if any left."

"A great many people have come in since that time."

"O yes; a great many."

"And didn't any of the old residents sell out to the new comers?"

"Yes; but not at that time."

Finding his grandmother positive on that branch of the subject, he tried another.

"Wasn't that about the time of the Indian troubles?"

"Well, it was after the worst of that."

"Wasn't there a great deal of feeling among the people on account of the war between the North and the South?"

"No; not particularly. Nearly all the people in this part of the country at that time were Southerners, but there was very great difference of sentiment."

"My father was a southern man?"

"Yes; but he never hurt anybody's feelings on that subject, because he never talked about it except to me and your mother; and we never repeated anything he said, as he always cautioned us against it, and said it would do no good to stir up bad blood."

"Grandmother, was anybody ever killed by Indians in this county?"

"Yes; several men were killed."

"Can you remember distinctly how many were killed after my father was murdered?"

"After your father was murdered? Let me see. That was in 1860, after the troubles were nearly all over. About a year after that, an old sheep-herder living near the foothills was killed by the Indians, and they stole his cattle."

"I have heard Uncle Dan speak of that," interrupted Nellie. "He was one of the men who went after the Indians, and I have heard him say that he helped to bury old Frenchie."

"You are sure of that, Nellie?" asked the young man— "sure that your father helped to bury him?"

"Yes; I have heard him tell how horribly the Indians mangled him."

This seemed to satisfy John, and he again turned his attention to his grandmother.

"Was anybody else killed?"

"Yes; two brothers named Webster—Henry and James Webster."

"When was that?"

"I think it was about a year after the old Frenchman was killed."

"The danger was greatest along the foothills, wasn't it?"

"Yes; they never troubled us away out here on the plains."

"Now, these men—these Websters: were they considered rich men?"

"Yes; at least, they had a great deal of land, but it was mortgaged, I believe."

"Were they married?"

"The older one—Henry—was married."

"Any children?"

"One, but it died."

"Where were the two brothers buried?"

"At that graveyard on this side of King's River, below the ford."

"Were you at the funeral?"

"Yes."

"Did you see the two men after they were killed?"

"No; they were too badly mutilated. It brought your father's death right back to my mind as plainly as if I saw it all over again."

"Who held the mortgage on their land?"

"I don't know."

"Who found them dead?"

"Well, it seems they were not found until after they had been dead several days. They even refused at first to let Mrs. Webster see her husband."

"Who refused?"

"The men who found the bodies."

"Who were those men?"

"I don't remember. Why, John, what in the world has all that to do with your father's death?"

"Perhaps nothing, grandmother; but I wish you would try to remember who found the bodies."

"Let me think. O, I remember now! They were some miners who had been prospecting for gold in the mountains, and they were coming down into the valley for provisions."

"Did anybody know them?"

"I can't say now, John."

"Did you see them?"

"No."

"Where was Mrs. Webster living at that time?"

"About two miles from my house. Don't you remember her?"

"Yes; I remember her very well now. You took me to the funeral with you. I was about nine years old."

"Exactly."

"If I remember correctly, grandmother, the miners, on finding the bodies, got some lumber somewhere, and made two rough coffins, and placed the Websters in them. Now, I want you to follow me closely, and correct any error I may make, for this is very important. The first thing they did after finding the bodies was to search the pockets for some means of identification, because the Websters were strangers to them; and besides, the faces of the dead men were perhaps unrecognizable. Am I right so far?"

"Perfectly; though I had forgotten some of that."

"They found letters, or some kind of documents, fixing the identity of the men and their place of residence, and then they hired a friendly Indian to carry the news to Mrs. Webster. Am I right?"

"Yes."

"They sent word to Mrs. Webster to send or bring a wagon in which the bodies could be taken home, and instructed the Indian to tell her that they would have the bodies in coffins by the time she arrived. Correct?"

"Yes."

"The messenger wanted to return with her, but she refused, as she was afraid of him, and she would not accept the services of any of the men in the neighborhood, telling them the miners would return from the mountains with her, and that she would not be afraid to go alone. The distance was about sixty miles—maybe sixty-five. She made the trip to the mountains and returned alone, the miners, for some reason, not having come. Am I correct again?"

"Perfectly correct. You have a splendid memory, John. But wasn't she a brave woman to make that terrible journey alone? I am sure I couldn't have done it."

"No, grandmother; you never could have done it," replied Graham, gravely and thoughtfully. Then he asked:

"What reputation did those men bear?"

"A very good one, so far as I know."

"Was there never anything against them?"

"Well, of course people will talk, you know. Some said they would take cattle from other people's bands, but I never believed a word of it."

"Let me see," said Graham: "Mrs. Webster left about a year after that, didn't she?"

"Yes."

"Do you know where she went?"

"To her people in Indiana, I think."

"And she has never been heard of since?"

"No. She promised to write to me, but she never did."

"How old were those men when they were killed?"

"Henry was, I should judge, about forty-two years of age, and James was two or three years younger."

"Describe them to me accurately, grandmother. I think I remember, but I want to see if your recollection agrees with mine."

"Henry was a tall, straight, fine-looking man. He had black hair, a straight, thin nose, dark eyes—"

"Brown, were they not?"

"Yes; brown, or a very dark blue."

"It was James who had dark blue eyes."

"You are right, John. It *was* James."

"Weren't Henry's eyes somewhat close together?"

"Yes. James was a shorter man, and not as good looking. His hair was not quite as dark as Henry's, and his eyes were large and farther apart, and he limped slightly on his left leg, as he broke it when he was a boy, and the bone was badly set."

"I think it was the right leg, grandmother."

"Sure enough! It was the right leg, for I remember that he was sparking the Widow Perkins; and she used to laugh, and say that his right leg would be left if he should run a race."

John had learned all he wanted to know, and the conversation came to a close. He escorted Nellie home, and was unusually grave and thoughtful. She tried her most winning subterfuges to make him cheerful, but she met with only defeat and chagrin. He stopped at the gate, and said:

"Nellie, will you come to-morrow, after you have finished your night's work, and stay with grandmother to-morrow night?"

"Are you going away, John?"

"Yes; but only for one night. Will you come?"

"Yes, if you will come for me."

"I will do that, certainly. And it's good of you to come, Nellie. I will reward you for it the day after to-morrow."

"How?"

"I will astonish you by telling you something very, very strange."

CHAPTER V.

A MIDNIGHT REVELATION.

THE sun was still high in the heavens when Graham tenderly kissed his grandmother and Nellie, telling them he would be out all night, and left the house. He saddled his horse, lashed a shovel to the pommel, and sallied out across the broad plains.

His thoughts took better shape in the quiet solitude that surrounded him, and that soothed his excited nerves. He felt that the murder, although admirably and indeed elaborately planned, could have been committed by none other than an amateur, for the simple reason that the murderer buried the money under Lone Tree. An experienced and skillful criminal would undoubtedly have escaped with the gold under cover of darkness. There was no doubt in his mind that the Lone Tree treasure was the fruit of his father's murder. The practiced highwayman would never have yielded to the demands of conscience, and told of the whereabouts of the gold; and this was additional foundation for the belief that an amateur did the work. The coincidence of dates and amounts was too singular for chance to be probable.

Aside from a discovery of the assassin, three problems presented themselves for solution: First, why was the treasure left undisturbed for nearly eighteen years? Second, why was it that the letter pointing out the Lone Tree secret came some months after the gold was removed? Third, why was the treasure taken up at all, and how could it have been done without the knowledge of the writer of the mysterious letter, who was evidently the murderer, desirous of making restitution and atonement so far as in his power lay? It would be an easy matter to say that the assassin had never possessed the courage to revisit the country and secure the gold: but how was it possible that so timid and cautious a man could have been overreached, as he evidently was, and without his knowledge? After all, there seemed to be no sympathy nor understanding whatever between the assassin and the priest who robbed Lone Tree of its treasure. They were independent of each other, and perhaps at cross-purposes. Here is one curious idea that forced itself upon John Graham's mind: would it be a brave and manly act to hunt down and wreak vengeance upon the murderer, when that man had done so redeeming and atoning a thing as to take all the steps he considered necessary to restore the fortune? Was not the dead man's blood washed away by that one wave of humanity? Was not the proper task before him a search for the treasure that was his by right, and just punishment to the man who ferreted out the secret of the iron pot? That act was baser than the murder itself, if that be possible; as in this case the criminal was a traitor, a thief, and a robber. But this man was a priest!

It must be borne in mind that Graham was unskilled in matters of the world, and had little knowledge of the darker side of human nature; also that he lacked quickness of perception and skill in methods, and that altogether he would have been utterly unfit for the task he had imposed upon himself, had he not possessed untiring patience, the power of continuous concentration of mind upon a particular subject, and an indomitable will. His conclusions were arrived at very slowly and cautiously; and even when they were thus formulated, he was not over-sanguine of their correctness. In some respects he was a remarkable man, else he could not have been the one to pass through such strange experiences as afterward fell to his lot.

After he had consumed about an hour in a brisk canter over the plains, a dark, low line, stretching as far as he could see on either hand, appeared to the northward, in place of the smooth line that had hitherto bounded the horizon. That which he now saw seemed almost black. This dark line was the timber that grows on the banks of King's River.

He now took a precaution. Heretofore he had traveled straight across the plains, thus saving much distance that he would have lost by traveling to the eastward, and finding and following a sinuous road to his destination. He supposed that he had been gradually nearing this road, and it became necessary to find it, especially as he soon became aware that a dreadful disturbance of the elements was threatened. An inexperienced observer would have overlooked these ominous signs; but Graham was familiar with the plains, and the strange occurrences of nature there. He knew the significance of every breath of air, and of every change in the temperature and direction of the winds. On this afternoon he said to himself:

"I must find the road, for the sand-storm is coming."

None who have ever witnessed this terrible phenomenon in the height of its fury will wonder that Graham felt some uneasiness.

"Let me see," he said: "I have not paid close enough attention to the direction in which I have been traveling. I am now within three miles of the river. Very good; but if I go straight ahead until I reach it, I may not know whether to turn to the right or to the left. I think I must be about two miles west of the road that leads to the ford. I must hurry."

After cogitating a few moments, he turned his horse slightly to the east, and took an oblique north-easterly course toward the river. This course considerably lengthened the distance between him and the river, as it was not a direct line thereto.

Graham spurred rapidly forward. He closely watched the line of trees, and presently he saw a dark reddish-gray wall looming up beyond the foliage. At the same time a brisk, cool breeze sprung up. This was the vanguard of the storm. Then a hoarse rumbling became audible, as the hurricane tore over the plains. The breeze freshened, and the trees in the distance were violently wrenched.

"Ah!" exclaimed Graham, in dismay. "I can't reach the road in time."

He turned his horse's head directly toward the trees, and

vigorously plied the spur. The trembling beast went rapidly on, with his nose close to the ground. Graham's intention was to reach the river as soon as possible, as the terrible cloud of sand would soon obliterate every landmark on the plains.

The rumbling changed to a bellowing. The furious storm rushed madly on—a storm without a cloud in the sky, but with one more terrible on the earth. In an incredibly short space of time, while Graham was still a considerable distance from the river, the sand-storm met him with terrific fury. He buttoned his coat to the chin, and pulled his hat far down. It was not a steady wind, but one of eddies and rushing whirlwinds. It discharged volley after volley of sweeping shrapnel, that sought every moment to unhorse the rider. It charged and enfiladed, tearing, uprooting, and scattering broadcast everything that stood in its way.

And that was not all. The sinking sun was blotted out, and his red rays imparted a somber glow to the cloud of driving sand that rushed headlong over the plains, and that besieged man and horse with pitiless fury. The line of trees had disappeared, and the horizon was gone. The ground beneath and a blank red glow around were all that could be seen through the impenetrable and all-pervading sand; which, driven at frightful speed, stung like the points of countless thousands of needles pricking the skin. This was the lash that the demon of the storm laid on, while he roared and bellowed with maddened anger. The horse could make no headway. Graham sent the spur home impatiently, and shouted; but his voice was lost in the roar of the storm, and the poor horse merely flinched when the spur was plied, refusing to move a step. Quivering in every muscle, the horse stood still, with drooped head and tail, and blinking his eyes as the stinging sand drove into them.

And that was not all. The wind cut the ground like a harrow, tearing up sage-brush and sending it whirling through the air. It uprooted the flowers in its giant strength, and scattered them over the plains. It tore along madly, finding victims here and there, and venting its full fury upon them. The ground heaved and rolled with moving waves of sand, like the sea in a storm.

It was a terrific storm. No thunder-storm could be more dreadful. It was swifter than a greyhound and stronger than a lion. It whisked and skimmed and dashed along; rushing and bounding and darting; nimble, yet strong; exploding like the crash of many cannon; wielding its bludgeon of sand—a catapult and a cudgel in one; violently riotous and fiercely wild; a tempest of rage and uproar; savage, ferocious, and frantic; thundering with impetuous turbulence; sharp, keen, and double-edged; fierce as a tiger; spreading havoc and desolation in its track; and ravaging and destroy- as if the Devil were in it.

In two hours it had spent its fury; and with one shake of its shaggy mane, it expired with a groan. The last straggling gusts, outstripped in the mad race with the stronger forces that had gone ahead, passed on, and a dead calm fell. But such a calm! The storm had left its trail of sand behind, like the straggling tail of a comet. The sun had set and the moon was up; but nothing could be seen but this silent and awful cloud of sand, that reached from the earth to the sky, shutting out everything from sight. Even the horse did not cast a shadow, though the moon was at the full. The warm glow that the setting sun had given to the cloud of sand was gone, and a pale yellow, spectral and feeble light remained —a weird, ghostly light, having not a suggestion of life, but cold and pallid, like death. After the roar came the silence, as of the grave.

The sand fell softly and noiselessly, like snow, and gathered on the rim of Graham's hat, and lodged on his shoulders and in creases in his clothes, and filtered through his horse's mane. If Graham opened his mouth and drew his breath, the sand would alight upon his tongue and be ground between his teeth.

But Graham was not idle. When the storm subsided, which was suddenly, he pushed on toward the river. As long as a straggling gust of wind remained, he knew the points of the compass, for the wind came from the north; but when the calm fell, and he found himself in this impenetrable cloud of falling sand, with no landmark visible by which to steer his course, he knew that he was in great danger. He did not fear the storm, for he could and did withstand its fury; but after the storm came the sand-cloud, which was infinitely more terrible than the storm.

On he rode through the gloom—on to the river. On he went, caring nothing that he dashed through stubborn sage and ran the risk of treacherous gopher-holes. The river, with its line of trees, lay just ahead, and in a moment he would reach it.

Strange to say, although he calculated after he had ridden some distance that the trees could be only a few steps away, and although he expected every moment to find some change in the contour of the ground indicating the near vicinity of the stream, yet he found no such change, and no sign of the trees. Still he pushed on, and still farther on; but the river did not appear.

A remarkable sensation is experienced on such an occasion. One knows a certain thing lies just ahead, and one knows the distance. When that distance is traversed, and more, and yet the thing sought is not found, one cannot help believing, in spite of any mental effort to the contrary, that the object has been removed.

"Egad!" exclaimed Graham, in dismay. "The river is gone!"

In other words, Graham was lost. Unconsciously he had turned out of the direction in which the river lay, and he might be three miles away. He could not see beyond his horse's ears, although there was no darkness, but only the yellow pallor of the sand-cloud.

He halted. It was useless to go farther at such a pace, which would soon take him twenty miles into the plains, in what direction he knew not. He sat and studied the problem a long time. Then a novel idea occurred to him.

"I have ridden the horse," he thought, "several hours, and he must be thirsty. If so, he will go toward the river if I give him the rein."

Graham tried the experiment. He dropped the rein and gently urged the horse. The animal took a few uncertain steps in the direction he faced, and then refused, in spite of Graham's urging, to go farther.

"This proves the course is wrong," thought Graham.

Then he turned the horse about, again dropped the rein, and gave a light touch with the spur. The animal started forward in the same uncertain manner as before, advanced a rod, and then came to a halt. Not only that, but he showed signs of the deepest fear. Evidently he realized that his master was lost, and instinct taught him to remain still until the sand-cloud should clear away. The signs of increased distress and fear showed themselves in the violent trembling of his legs and flank, and in an occasional loud snorting, and in a high raising of the head and pricking up of the ears.

Graham saw that this plan was not feasible. Then he carefully studied the situation.

"If my mind had been less troubled," he thought, "I shouldn't have fallen into this bad scrape."

He put aside his preoccupation; and no sooner had he succeeded in this effort than a thought, startling for its suddenness, occurred to him.

Then he dismounted, and taking the bridle in his hand, commenced to study the ground narrowly.

"I might have known," he muttered, "that the weeds lean from the river."

The explanation of this phenomenon lies in the fact that the storm, coming from the north, caused all vegetable growth to incline to the south. As he was south of the river, the weeds must lean in a direction contrary to that in which the river lay. Having thus found the proper direction, he mounted his horse, proceeded a few rods slowly, and then dismounted to observe the weeds. He corrected his course from the slight deviation into which he had fallen, remounted, and proceeded. He repeated this several times, and had progressed a mile or more, when his horse stumbled over a hillock, and then abruptly halted.

"This is the bank of the river," said Graham, with elation.

He dismounted and carefully examined the hillock. It had an unusual shape, and, strange to say, was unaccountably softer than the surrounding hard ground. It was about seven feet long, and tapering small at the ends.

"I don't understand it," muttered Graham. "This can't be the river bank."

The matter was one deserving close scrutiny; and so Graham tethered his horse to a scrubby bunch of sage, and commenced an investigation. The sand-cloud was so dense, and the obscuration of the moon so complete, that Graham, standing at one end of the mysterious hillock, could not see the other end. He went around it to the other side, and had taken but two or three steps when he discovered another mound very similar to the other, the difference being that the second was smaller and firmer than the first, and some wild-flowers grew on it. He passed this one, and at a distance equal to that between the others, he found a third, but it was much shorter.

The darkness was so inpenetrable that he could not see these hillocks, or mounds, until his feet encountered them, and on coming to one he would stumble and nearly fall.

He passed the third mound—or, more properly, ridge—and suddenly floundered in a high and irregular pile of soft, loose dirt, evidently thrown up recently. He sank to his shoe tops, and pulled through to the other side. As he did so, not suspecting that it ended abruptly, he pitched forward, turned suddenly to regain his footing, failed, and then dextrously made a leap for the firm ground beyond. Instead of succeeding in that, he plunged headlong into an abyss.

He struck the bottom with a hollow, heavy thud, and lay for a moment half stunned. He had fallen about six feet. He attempted to regain his feet, but his head and shoulder struck a wall of dirt. He glanced upward, and saw through the mouth of a hole a little over six feet long and a little less than three feet wide, into which he had tumbled, the pale yellow sand-cloud between him and the sky. He put out his hands, and felt the walls of the hole. They were smooth and straight. He stood up, grasped the edge of the opening, and was almost in the act of springing to the surface, when a ghastly realization burst upon him.

"I am in a grave!" he whispered half aloud.

The horror of the situation momentarily paralyzed his arm, and a cold, creeping chill passed down his back. With an agile strength, rendered doubly strong by the fear that for a moment possessed him, he sprung nimbly to the surface. In another moment all his self-possession had returned, and he was half inclined to laugh at his fright.

As a sequence to this realization came another.

"Ah!" he exclaimed, "I am in a burying-ground—the very one I was hunting for."

The relief that he experienced from this reflection was almost exhilarating. In order to assure himself that his opinion was correct, he reflected a moment; then gathered up the stems of a few dead weeds, produced a match, and soon had a small blaze kindled. The light thus produced enabled him to find other sticks; and in a short time he had a cheery little fire crackling in the graveyard. He got his bearings from two or three head-boards that he recognized; and, as the river was only a few steps away, he went toward it, carrying a small torch to light his way, and presently returned with an armful of dry branches from the willows. With these he made a considerable fire. He brought his horse within the small circle of light, secured the halter to a sickly tree standing at the head of a neglected grave, unlashed the shovel, and proceeded about the work before him.

The red glare of the fire imparted a ruddy hue to the sand-cloud, whose whiteness then seemed tinged with blood.

Arming himself with a torch, he sought carefully among the scattered graves, patiently deciphering the half-obliterated inscriptions on the painted boards.

Presently his efforts were rewarded.

"This is it," he said, as he pushed the shovel into the mound over a grave.

He carefully noted the surroundings, went back to the fire, and returned with some fagots he had held in reserve. With these he made another fire close to the grave he had selected.

Then he threw off his coat and hat, and assailed the mound with his shovel. It was an old grave, and badly neglected. The board at the head, being of redwood, was well preserved.

In a moment the mound had disappeared, and it lay in a heap on one side. He worked furiously, throwing out the dirt with great rapidity. He was down two feet, then three, then four.

Suddenly the point of the shovel struck something hard at the bottom. He worked with greater care, fearing the boards were rotten. He removed all the dirt that his shovel could reach; then he sprung to the surface, and moved the fire to that side of the pile of dirt nearest the grave. In this manner he succeeded in throwing a very good light into the grave, but it did not reach the bottom, as the wall nearest the fire prevented.

He went down into the grave again, and carefully removed one of the loose boards that covered the coffin. He found these boards in a fair state of preservation. He took up one of these.

The coffin appeared to his view. He could see that, as it was pine, which is not nearly so durable as redwood, it was very rotten, and ready to fall to pieces.

He reached around and grasped the shovel, and carefully inserted the edge of the blade under the coffin lid. The soft wood yielded, hardly without resistance.

Then he laid the shovel aside, knelt down, slipped his fingers underneath the end of the lid, and gave a steady pull. The board yielded like rotten paper, and broke short off about two feet from the end.

At that moment, when the object of Graham's search lay just under his eyes, the blaze suddenly expired, and he found himself in total darkness.

An indefinable fear, an intense loathing, and the unutterable horror of the situation, sent a sudden shock through his frame.

But he was a brave man, and was, above all things, intensely stubborn. Through spite and sheer force of will, he overcame the timidity that threatened to overpower him, and mincingly began to feel around with his hand. It found the edge of the coffin, and very carefully and very slowly it traversed the distance to the bottom. He remained in that attitude nearly half a minute, and his hand was not idle.

Then he withdrew his hand, replaced the boards, emerged from the grave, lighted the fire, and stood upon the ground, staring wildly around, with a terrible look in his face, in which were mingled fierce anger and a desperate hate.

He refilled the grave, placing the headboard again in proper position, rounded over the mound, put on his hat and coat, picked up the shovel, remounted his horse, found the road, and plied the spur. The sand-cloud had passed, and the night was beautiful.

The first tinge of dawn was warming the sky over Miners' Peak, when he softly rapped at his grandmother's door. The good old lady welcomed him home, but asked him no questions. He spoke gently to her, and called "Good night" cheerily to Nellie.

"It is good morning, John," she replied.

Laughing at the sally, he passed on to his own room, and was soon in a dead sleep from utter exhaustion.

When he emerged from his room at noon that day, the first thing he said was:

"Nellie, do you remember that I promised to tell you something strange to-day, as a reward for your staying with grandmother last night?"

"Yes," replied Nellie, dying with curiosity.

"But before I tell you, I want to strike another bargain with you."

"What is it, John?"

"That we postpone our wedding until I am rich."

A dubious look came into her face, but it was followed by a sparkle in the eye as she asked:

"Will it be long?"

"Less than a year, I hope—may be longer; but we are young, and I shall have another strong incentive to carry out my determination."

"Very well, John," she answered, with a pretty look of resignation, and with a well-feigned sigh.

"And now for that something strange I promised to tell you. Grandmother, listen attentively to what I am going to say. I want you also to know it."

"Well, John, I am listening."

"I know who murdered my father," he said quietly.

They stared at him in speechless astonishment.

CHAPTER VI.

A STRANGE VISITOR.

JOHN GRAHAM had undergone a wonderful transformation within the last four days. Into that short space had been crowded hope, ambition, anger, and despair, to an extent seldom felt throughout the whole span of one man's natural life. He was broken, but not seasoned. The hardening would come with time, and a continuation of the anxieties that had recently harassed him. He was no longer a boy; but was not yet a man, in the sense of manhood equal to a battle with dire emergencies. The timidity of the boy was gone; and the bold, daring, resolute man stood revealed. By an accident, he had discovered his strength; but this brought him no pride nor vanity. Indeed, he did not even know he had undergone so great a change. If his thoughts entered that channel at all, they perceived only the apparent fact that it was outward things and circumstances that had suffered any change, and that their bearing upon him called for the exercise of all the sterner stuff in his nature. Vanity was a stranger to this man. He was proud, almost to the extent of scorn; but his pride was healthful, elevating, and ennobling. It was pride in a clean conscience and unsullied honor, and pride in consistency in right action, and pride in yielding not an inch to wrong, but in pursuing it to the ends of the earth.

He was fortunate in the possession of great patience. It would have been a difficult matter to cause him to be carried away with some pet scheme that did not have a grand result in view. His nature was large and roomy, and it was proportionately strong and durable. It might have been better for him had he been endowed with greater caution; but the absence of unusual prudence was more than compensated for by his daring, which would carry by storm what could as well be accomplished by strategy.

He remained inactive at home for an entire week, studying his plans, learning by heart every incident that had passed, and quietly making inquiries here and there. Having put everything in readiness for his departure, and having made arrangements for his grandmother's stay at the home of Nellie's uncle for a few days, he provided himself with a little money from the hoard in his grandmother's keeping, mounted his horse, and struck out across the plains.

He crossed King's River, skirted the northern shore of Tulare Lake, crossed the parched desert beyond, penetrated the Coast Range, emerged on the western side through Pacheco Pass, entered the broad, beautiful valley between the Coast Range and the Santa Cruz Mountains, turned northward, passed through Gilroy and San Jose, skirted the Bay of San Francisco on the west, and arrived at San Francisco, three hundred miles from home.

It was the first time he had ever seen a city; yet so even was his organization, and so readily could he adapt himself to circumstances, that he was not seriously, if at all, bewildered. He asked necessary directions in an easy manner, and had a straightforward way and a dignity of bearing that won him respect. He felt at home in any street, and found his way without difficulty or embarrassment. Two weeks ago he could not have done it.

In due time he presented himself to the chief of police.

"Can you tell me," asked Graham, "where I may find a man who will undertake a difficult piece of detective work for a heavy fee—which, however, must be contingent?"

"Hump!" grunted that worthy functionary. "They are generally contingent."

"You know the men engaged in such business, and you would place me under many obligations by recommending a man equal to the task."

"What is the nature of the job?"

"I want to find a man who committed a murder eighteen years ago."

The detective gave a long whistle.

"But I don't see anything contingent in that," urged the chief.

"The murderer was also a robber."

"I see."

"By the murder he secured a large sum of money."

"Exactly. How much?"

"Twenty-two thousand dollars."

"Twenty-two thousand dollars!" echoed the chief, in astonishment.

"That money is mine by right," continued the young man.

"I see."

"And I will give five thousand dollars of it to the man who finds the murderer."

"Exactly; but suppose the murderer hasn't the money."

"I know he hasn't."

"O, you do!"

"Certainly."

"Then how can you recover the money?"

"The murderer knows who has the money."

"That's a good idea," grunted the chief. "I will think the matter over, and try to find you some man equal to the case."

The young man returned to his lodgings, the chief saying he would send a man the following day.

The next day a man rapped at Graham's door.

"You are the detective whom the chief was to send, I suppose?" asked Graham, bluntly. "Come in. Sit down. What is your name?"

Graham did not notice a slight abashment in the man's manner, produced, possibly, by the direct, frank, and business-like welcome of the young man.

The stranger seated himself on the proffered chair, not yet having spoken a word, and handed Graham a card, on which was printed:

J. V. COVILL,
PRIVATE DETECTIVE.

"I am glad to know you, Mr. Covill," said Graham. "Do you want to undertake this case?"

"Well," said the man, drawing a deep breath of relief, "we'll talk it over, and see what there is in it. I must know all about it, you see, before I can have any idea whether or not it will pay me to undertake it. You don't propose to put up any money on it, do you?"

"Not a cent."

"That makes it rather bad, you understand; because I might spend what little money I have, and then not accomplish anything."

"If that's your disposition, I had better look for another man."

"O, you are in too big a hurry! When you've been in the business as long as I have, you'll learn a little caution— that's all. I simply want to know something about the case. As I understand it, the murder was committed a great many years ago."

"Eighteen years."

"That's a long time, you know. The chances are that the man is dead."

"No; he's alive."

"You seem to know who did it," exclaimed the detective, in astonishment.

"I do know."

"Oh!" ejaculated Covill. He looked at the young man with the keenest interest, and with a surprise that he did not attempt to conceal.

"How long have you known it?" he asked.

"That is no matter," replied Graham, sharply and sternly.

Covill was evidently uneasy. He had to deal with a man more than his match in nerve and will.

"Then you don't propose to tell me all you know?" inquired Covill, in tones of deep respect, but with a certain awkwardness, as if he feared an unpleasant explosion at any moment. Graham eyed him steadily and sternly; and with a barely perceptible tinge of scorn in his voice, he answered:

"I will tell you what I please to tell you, and nothing more. I will tell you all that is necessary for you to know. I will throw nothing in your way, but will assist all I can. If you undertake this case, I shall expect you to follow any instructions I choose to give you."

Covill saw that he had a man before him who would bear not the least trifling; who feared nothing, and who respected no unnecessary scruples; whom Covill could manage no more successfully than he could a grizzly bear at bay.

"Well," said Covill, after a long pause, "tell me what you can then, and I shall see what can be done."

Graham readily assented. He gave a history of the murder and of the search for the treasure, and then he stopped.

"Is that all?" asked Covill, evidently disappointed.

Graham remained silent a minute in deep thought.

"How did you know the treasure was buried at the foot of Lone Tree?" asked Covill respectfully.

"I had thought," musingly replied Graham, "not to tell you, but I now believe it is best you should know."

"It is absolutely necessary," said Covill.

"Not absolutely, but it may be better. I feel that I am reposing great confidence in you, and I rely on you to keep these matters to yourself."

"Certainly."

Graham produced the mysterious letter. The detective read it carefully, and his eyes sparkled. He folded the letter, and was in the act of placing it in his pocket-book, when Graham's hand stayed him.

"You can't have that letter," said Graham, firmly.

The detective slightly flushed with anger, but offered no opposition.

"But this is the only clew I have," urged Covill, with some warmth; "and I can't take a single step without it. Don't you see that the writer of this letter is, beyond doubt, the murderer?"

"I know it," quietly responded Graham; "but he is only one of them."

"One of them?"

"Yes; there are two."

"Oh!" exclaimed Covill, leaning back helpless in his chair, and regarding the young man with an indescribable look of astonishment and wonder.

"Besides," continued Graham, "there's a third person— the priest. And then, if you are anything of a detective, you ought to know that the writer of this letter will learn that I failed to find the treasure, and that therefore he has been balked in his design by some one who has played fast and loose with him, and that he will surely, beyond the possibility of a doubt, let me hear from him again, and that very soon. But he will not disclose his whereabouts. Hence I want help."

The detective was crushed and dejected. The superiority of Graham over him, and the high hand and absolute confidence with which he carried off this advantage, made the detective feel uncomfortable and insignificant. Happening at last to observe in Covill's face traces of these feelings, Graham silently pondered over the matter, and then said:

"Don't think that I am to be contrary and unreasonable. I have no doubt you are a skillful man, or the chief never would have sent you to me. Possibly I seem to you to be abrupt and harsh. I don't intend to be. The reason I am so positive concerning certain things is, that I have given those things the very closest study. I don't pretend to be a detective; but the conclusions I have come to are so natural that you yourself could not avoid them, knowing as much as I know."

The detective's face gradually cleared during the progress of this frank speech, which brought the two men nearer together, and placed them upon an even footing.

"As I was saying," continued Graham, "we may naturally expect to hear again from the writer of that letter. It seems to me that there cannot possibly be anything in common between the writer and the priest. I think it is probable that the other of the two murderers was the source of information to the priest, who I don't believe was a priest at all."

Another quick look of surprise darted across the detective's face. He instantly recovered himself, and the conversation proceeded. After it had continued a few minutes, the detective said:

"I will undertake the case."

"Very well."

"And am I to have five thousand dollars if I arrest the man?"

"Yes."

"Is that all that's to be done?"

"No; the priest must be found."

"And is that all?"

"That is all. When you have done that much, I will relieve you, and will finish the job myself."

He said this very quietly, and the puzzled and searching look with which the detective regarded him failed to reveal anything but a deep determination of some kind.

The conversation ceased. Graham had already given the detective the names and description of the two murderers. After some moments of silence the detective said calmly:

"I think you are on the wrong scent."

"How is that?"

"You have entirely overlooked one important thing."

"Well?"

"The man who wrote that letter is evidently a Catholic."

"Why so?"

"I'll prove it: the letter shows on its face that he has repented of the murder, and wants to do all he can to repair the evil effects of it."

"Undoubtedly."

"A man who has such a disposition requires a confidant."

'Evidently."

"It is apparent that this crime has for some time been weighing heavily on his mind."

"Possibly; but what makes you think so?"

Encouraged at the keen interest he had aroused in Graham, the detective's face brightened, all his assurance returned, and he continued in a tone of the most positive conviction:

"There can be no doubt about it. The inference is unavoidable. You are not the only person he has taken into his confidence."

"Indeed?"

"Yes. He made up his mind to be a good man, and naturally desired forgiveness. As that was out of the question, he resorted to a course very much like it."

"And what was that?"

"Absolution."

"Absolution!"

"Yes."

"But I don't understand you," said Graham, eagerly and greatly confused.

"He joined the Catholic Church, which is the only one that grants absolution."

"Well?"

"He went to a priest, resolved to begin a new life, and made a full confession of all his past crimes and shortcomings."

The light was dimly breaking upon Graham's mind.

"He confessed this murder to the priest, and told of the robbery and the buried treasure. The priest's heart bounded, and he trembled in every limb—"

"What is your theory?" interrupted Graham, impatiently.

"The priest extorted from the murderer a confession as to the spot where the treasure was buried. Then the priest absolved him and blessed him; and then, yielding to a temptation too strong for human nature, he procured a horse and buggy, started out in search of the gold, found it, and hid it."

Graham certainly was excited. He was on his feet before Covill had finished, and breathed deep and hard.

"You must be right," he said in a half whisper. "Strange I had not thought of it before!"

"Now, give me a description of the priest with minute accuracy."

Graham complied in a dazed, helpless way.

"Keep quiet a few days," added Covill, "and I am certain I can find the priest."

"Very well."

"When will you return?"

"I will stay here a few days longer."

"Good day. You shall hear from me again."

"Good day."

The detective had left the room, when he remembered something forgotten, and then returned to the door.

"Probably," he said, "another detective will come to see you about this matter. Of course it will never do to let another man into this case without my consent."

"Certainly not."

"Good day."

"Good day."

Graham sat in a kind of half stupor nearly an hour, when his reverie was interrupted by a rap at the door.

"Come in."

A stranger, calm, dignified, and self-possessed, entered in obedience to the summons.

"Good afternoon, sir," he said gravely. "I was informed by the chief of police that you want the services of a detective in an important and obscure case."

"I have already secured a man."

"Ah!"

The stranger was surprised. He shrugged his shoulders, and with his grave, dignified manner, said:

"Then you have no need of my services."

"None whatever."

"Good afternoon, sir."

"Good afternoon."

In the mean time Covill went his way with a light step and a self-satisfied air. In three minutes he arrived at a stairway, mounted two steps at a time, rapped at a door, and entered. The room in which he stood, hat in hand, was a cozy private room adjoining the elegantly appointed study-room of a lawyer. A tall, white-haired man sat in an easy-chair, and asked Covill to seat himself. Covill's manner had undergone a strange change from the moment he rapped at the door. In place of the buoyancy, he seemed jaded and haggard. Before seating himself he closed the door leading into the study-room.

"Well?" said the old man, inquiringly.

"I made it, Judge, but he's the hardest man to tackle that I ever saw."

"But you succeeded?"

"Yes: after a harder fight than I want to have again soon, I got him under my thumb. But he's terribly ugly. By George! if I had known what kind of a man he is, I wouldn't have commenced this job for a thousand dollars. I am willing to draw out of it now, and not charge you a cent for what I have done; but I'll see myself dead before I'll consent to carry this dirty job out for two hundred dollars, as we agreed the other day. I must have five hundred dollars, or I don't move a peg."

"I'll make it a thousand," quietly remarked the old man.

It was about this time that the second detective who visited Graham remarked to the chief:

"That young fellow has employed a man."

"That is strange," replied the chief; "for I sent no man but you to him. I suppose he picked up somebody."

CHAPTER VII.

NELLIE'S NEW FRIENDS.

THERE had been a mild winter, and the spring had opened unusually early. The rains had ceased. They had been light, and the farmers felt considerable uneasiness for fear the crops would be a partial failure. Particularly was this the case in the San Joaquin Valley, where other discouraging influences operate than the uncertainty of the seasons. There were artificial obstacles as well as those that were natural.

Still, an early spring was hailed joyfully by tourists—that vast swarm of human bees that desert the busy hives in summer, and go out to enjoy the fresh, perfumed air of the plains.

A few days after Graham left for San Francisco, a merry party of pleasure seekers left the railroad at a station in Tulare County, and from persons living there, with whom arrangements had previously been effected, procured large wagons, in which to take a trip to Tulare Lake. Its shore is covered with a dense growth of tules, and there is an utter absence of inspiring scenery. Nevertheless, it possesses some remarkable features, one of which being that it is the greatest resort of water-fowl in the State, wild ducks and geese abounding in countless numbers. The time of year at which the tourists found themselves on the plains of Tulare County was well selected. The gentlemen of the party could find no better sport than shooting wild geese; while the women could amuse themselves with the excellent fishing that the waters of the lake afford.

The presence of the great numbers of geese often presents a remarkable sight, and one well worth seeing. They cover the ground like snow, and when disturbed they take wing, with the noise of a rushing storm. It was for such sights as these that the party of tourists proposed to visit the lake—an unusual trip, but one offering many inducements.

The party consisted of four men and as many women— all well-bred, well-to-do people from San Francisco. Some of them were young and unmarried.

"This is glorious!" exclaimed one pretty and vivacious young lady, as she stood on the veranda of the little hotel at sunrise, and gazed wonderingly at the mirage on the plains to the northward. "This surely *can't* be a mirage! Why, there are beautiful tall palms standing on such pretty little green islands, and such smooth, glassy water all around, and the dark green trees away, away on the farther side! O Auntie, surely that is not the dread mirage we read about, that leads the thirsty traveler onward, and that finally melts away, leaving only the desert before and behind and all around! It is as natural as life, and more beautiful than anything I ever saw before. Did you ever see anything half so grand, Auntie?"

"I have seen the mirage often, my child—not here," said the elder woman, correcting herself with some haste—"not here, but on the desert, when your uncle and I came overland to California. You remember that trip, don't you? It was ten years ago, and you were six years old then."

"I can barely remember it. I think it is good of Uncle Frank to let us come down here instead of sending us to Yosemite, don't you, Aunt?"

"Yes, Alice," replied the aunt, but with a preoccupied air.

The other members of the party came tripping gayly out from the breakfast-table.

"O Mr. Edwards!" exclaimed Alice. "Come and see the beautiful mirage! Why—why—Auntie, it is gone! Where is it?"

Her artless surprise and disappointment amused the man.

"See, Alice," he laughingly said, "the sun has just peeped over the Sierra, and the mirage is frightened away."

The lovely girl gazed dreamily out upon the plains, endeavoring to stamp ineffaceably on her memory the gorgeous picture she had seen.

They laughed and chatted, like children out of school, and ran about on the plains, gathering great armfuls of bright wild flowers; exclaiming when they found one more beautiful than the others, and exhibiting triumphantly every rare floral trophy. Nothing half so bewitching had they ever seen in the exotic gardens of the city. Surely these whilom wind-swept, desolate plains—the abode of the gopher, and the sleepy owl that was his companion, and the

Many of the most successful and competent Teachers on this Coast negotiate for positions through this agency. We supply many of the best schools, both public and private, with principals, and assistants in English Branches, Mathematics, Natural Sciences, Ancient and Modern Languages, Vocal and Instrumental Music, Drawing and Painting, Gymnastics, Military Tactics, etc. Many families secure Tutors and Governesses through our aid.

School authorities will please state what salary will be paid, the grade of school, time of opening, certificate required, cost of board, etc.

Having no favorites to provide for, an impartial and conscientious effort will be made to secure the best interests of our patrons.

The Bureau is indorsed by our prominent educators, among whom are the following:—

Hon. F. M. Campbell, State Superintendent.
Dr. John LeConte, President of the University of California
Hon. John Swett, Ex-State Superintendent and Principal of the San Francisco Girls' High School
Prof. Charles H. Allen, Principal of the State Normal School

Address all communications to

MYRON H. SAVAGE, & CO. MANAGERS,

PACIFIC BUREAU OF EDUCATION,

19 NEW MONTGOMERY STREET,

SAN FRANCISCO, CAL.

Commercial Law—Relating to Negotiable Paper, Contracts, Partnerships, etc.
Business Customs—Lectures and practical instruction on business customs, etc.
Lectures and Instruction—On Commercial Geography, Political Economy, etc.

RATES OF TUITION.

SCHOLARSHIP for the full Business Course as above explained, time unlimited - **$70**
Three Months, Day Sessions . . . . $45 | Three Months, Evening Sessions . . . $25
One Month " " . . . . 18 | One Month " " . . . 10

ACADEMIC COURSE.

This Course is designed for imparting to persons of any age thorough instruction in the ordinary English branches, such as Spelling, Reading, Writing, Arithmetic, Grammar, Composition, Letter-Writing, History, etc.; and the General Mathematical branches, such as Higher Arithmetic, Algebra, Geometry, Mensuration, Surveying, Civil Engineering, Navigation, etc.

RATES OF TUITION: Six Months, $45; Three Months, $25; One Month, $10.

COMBINED COURSE.

It is frequently desirable for students taking the Business Course to combine with it one or more of the studies of the Academic Course. Where the studies of the two courses are combined, the charge per term of six months is $70.

TELEGRAPHIC COURSE.

This course offers unsurpassed facilities for learning Telegraphy. Air Lines, Relays, Sounders, Switches, etc., with all the apparatus to be found in any telegraph office, are used; so that students can become good operators in the shortest possible time.

RATES OF TUITION: Six Months, $40; Three Months, $25; One Month, $10.
Students of the Commercial or Academical Departments will be charged the following rates: Six Months, $25; Three months, $15; One Month, $6.
NOTE—Students taking the Business Course or the Combined Course, receive instruction in the *Modern Languages*, *Free of Charge*.

NO VACATIONS—DAY AND EVENING SESSIONS DURING THE ENTIRE YEAR.

Oakland Daily Times Job Print, 950 Broadway.

PACIFIC BUSINESS COLLEGE

320 POST STREET,

SAN FRANCISCO.

RED MEN'S BUILDING,
Opposite Union Square,

This School is justly ranked by the public as the best Commercial College on the Pacific Coast. It offers to both sexes superior facilities in the following courses of instruction:

THE BUSINESS COURSE.

This is designed to prepare students for BUSINESS PURSUITS. It embraces:

Book-keeping—BY BOTH SINGLE AND DOUBLE ENTRY, as applied to all kinds of business, such as Wholesale and Retail Merchandising, Farming, Manufacturing, Mining, Brokerage and Exchange, Importing and Jobbing, Commission, Railroading, Banking, Etc.

Commercial Calculations—Embracing the most rapid and abbreviated methods of calculation in Percentage, Profit and Loss, Commission, Interest and Discount, Domestic and Foreign Exchange, General Average, Equation of Payments, Interest Accounts, Averaging Accounts, Partnership Settlements, etc.

Penmanship—Including careful instruction in the finger, muscular, whole-arm and combined movements, as applied to plain business writing, ledger headings, etc.

Correspondence—Embracing instruction in composition of business letters, use of capitals, rules of punctuation, folding, addressing, etc.

Business Forms—Such as Notes, Drafts, Bills of Exchange, Accounts Current,

PACIFIC
BUREAU of EDUCATION

MYRON H. SAVAGE & CO., MANAGERS,

19 New Montgomery St., San Francisco.

SCHOOLS SUPPLIED WITH TEACHERS WITHOUT EXPENSE.

Trustees of Public Schools and Principals of Private Schools should correspond *with us* before engaging Teachers.

Teachers who want positions, or who wish to change location, should send for "*application form,*" inclosing stamp.

For Schools of every grade, from primary to collegiate, the Bureau has facilities for furnishing Teachers holding the highest cer-

screaming hawk, and the broad-winged eagle—surely this boundless, dried-up sea, with its deep, productive soil, and its beautiful tree-lined streams, was the garden spot of all the lands over which the winds from the Pacific passed—a place where the bountiful blessings of nature should be enjoyed; where health, wealth, and happiness should be the lot of men; where men sowed the grain, and women milked the cows, and children gathered wild-flowers from the plains —surely human avarice should not mar this handiwork of God, and lurk in the darkness, like a thief, and set man against man, and neighbor against neighbor, and husband against wife, and father against son; and lay traps, and set snares, and trip the unwary, and make cowards of brave men; and rob the poor, and hinder the thrifty, and cajole its misguided friends—surely these noble plains, lying under the full light that pours straight down from heaven, should not be cursed with the hand of the rich on the throat of the poor; with the robber rolling in princely wealth, itself outstripping in magnificence the hidden treasure of Monte Cristo, and flinging this insult in the face of man and the teeth of God—*What are you going to do about it?*

Can a man raise wheat? Well enough; for the ground is rich and the soil is deep. Can he sell it? Well enough; for a hungry world holds out its hand for the harvest from these plains. Can he reap a profit? Why not?—for cheap is the land, and little is the work that this paradise demands. *Does* he reap a profit? God, no! for his costs are weighed, and his gains are pared to the quick.

Well, *what will you do about it?* Nothing. Nothing.

Absolutely nothing. Sit down and whine like a cur whose tail has been stepped on; unresistingly be bullied and trodden under foot; tremble under the frown of imperious arrogance, and lick the boot that drives the stinging kick; grovel in poverty, and sleep with gaunt hunger; laugh and sing, and eat and be merry, like leering louts, like driveling idiots, like brainless fools; and dance, though the fiddler be Death.

That is what is done about it, and that is all that will be done about it, until *men* are born and cowards are kicked aside.

The wagons soon were ready. There were two, and they were large and roomy. Mrs. Harriott (for such was the name of Alice's aunt, who exercised a kind of maternal supervision over the entire party) had wisely foreseen many of the difficulties and inconveniences that would be met with on the trip, and had already sent out a messenger, charged with making preparations at farm-houses for dinner and supper for the party. Acting under the instruction of Mrs. Harriott, the messenger made arrangements for dinner at the house of Nellie's uncle.

This Mrs. Harriott was a woman of unusual strength of character. This was seen in her large, sinewy hands, in her firm compression of the lips, her square shoulders and erect carriage, and the steady glance of her eyes. She was a woman to be depended on in a test of nerve and discretion. She must have been at least fifty years of age, although a stranger would not have supposed she was over forty. She had cool self-possession, and would be at ease under any circumstances. Nevertheless, there was a certain steely look in her eyes—a certain dangerous and uncompromising coldness—that would forever prevent her becoming the confidential friend of a sympathetic person. She displayed an unobtrusive but surprisingly accurate knowledge of all the common affairs of every-day life, under many of its varied aspects. She was as much at home on the plains as she was in her reception room in San Francisco. She knew the name of every weed and flower. This one was poisonous, that one fragrant. This flower was a bluebell, that a columbine, the other a poppy, still another a lupin, and so on through the list. She was familiar with the mountains, and entertained the party with descriptions of Mt. Tyndal, Mt. Whitney, Mt. Kaweah, and Miner's Peak. She had a quiet, dignified air, that commanded attention and respect. Alice, be it said, was an adopted child, although she did not employ parental appellations.

It was a happy day for all the party, excepting, perhaps, Mrs. Harriott, whose manner was by habit too stern and composed to permit any exhibition of enjoyment or any other feeling.

At noon they arrived at Foster's. Nellie, fluttering with excitement at this hitherto unheard-of episode in her quiet life on the plains, and feeling on her shapely shoulders the whole weight of responsibility that the occasion imposed, had made careful preparation for the reception of the party, not overlooking certain primitive but effective secrets of good taste in the matter of her own fresh personal appearance. Her eyes sparkled and her cheeks glowed with exercise and excitement when she went to the gate, followed by her slower uncle, to welcome the strangers. While Mr. Foster cared for the horses, Nellie ushered the party into the house, volubly disparaging the accommodations she offered, and blushing prettily under the shower of compliments that especially the gentlemen of the party heaped upon her.

When Mr. Foster appeared at the gate, Mrs. Harriott eyed him narrowly, and then her attention was directed to Nellie. She warmed to the girl in a manner entirely foreign to her usual way. She complimented Nellie's fine black hair, her large blue eyes, her rosy-white complexion, her dimpled cheeks, and her pretty mouth. Nellie laughed, blushed, and chattered. She had never felt half so happy in all her life before. The sensation of being with these bright, witty people was novel, exhilarating, almost intoxicating. And let it be said—and not at all to Nellie's discredit—that she was by no means abashed in their presence; that she gave repartee for sally, and laughed heartily at them for their ignorance of country ways; and she made the men stare in open-mouthed wonder, as she in an offhand manner recounted her daring exploits on the wildest mustang ponies in the country.

There never was a dinner half so jolly, and there were never appetites keener or more appreciative, and there never was a dinner more fit for a king. So agreeably did the time slip away, that two hours had already passed since the arrival—two hours of precious time. Strange that so cool and calculating a woman as Mrs. Harriott should have yielded to the sweet seductions of that pleasant home!

There was another person in whom Mrs. Harriott took great interest—Graham's grandmother. The poor old lady was dazed by the noise and overflow of spirits that the happy party brought into the house, and she would have been glad to run surreptitiously away to her own deserted home; but Mrs. Harriott found good opportunity to pay many kind attentions to the old lady, and engaged her in conversation apart from the others, and listened with the keenest interest to Mrs. Graham's recital of her troubles, and her love for her grandson, whom the old lady solemnly asserted to be the noblest boy that ever lived. With judiciously framed interrogatories she learned every iota of Graham's movements, discoveries, and intentions that the old lady knew.

Calling Nellie aside, she thanked the girl in the tenderest, most earnest manner; and before Nellie could realize what had happened, she found upon her wrist a heavy bracelet of rich, yellow, woven gold, and the solid ends of the graceful spiral were set each with a handsome pearl and turquois. It was the most magnificent piece of jewelry that had ever come under the wrapt gaze of Nellie.

She turned deathly pale.

"Wear it, Nellie," said Mrs. Harriott, "as a memento of this day, which has been such a happy one."

Nellie partially recovered from her stupor of surprise, and then threw herself upon Mrs. Harriott's neck, and kissed her again and again, and then sank down on a chair, and cried piteously from pure excess of joy. Mrs. Harriott soothed her in the kindest manner, and presently Nellie's equanimity was restored. Mrs. Harriott then passed her arm through Nellie's and carried her back to the party, the members of which were lounging in chairs on the veranda; and Mrs. Harriott, addressing Mr. Foster and the tourists, said:

"Mr. Foster, I have a proposition to make to you, and one that I am sure will be heartily seconded by everybody present. It is that you permit Nellie to accompany us to the lake, and remain with us in camp."

This second surprise completely took the breath from Nellie. The members of the party all joined clamorously in the request; and before Nellie could say a word, Mr. Foster had yielded under the storm that assailed him, and he gave his consent. It is unnecessary to say that Nellie was only too happy to join the party. By the time her hasty preparations were completed the wagons were ready to start; and then they sallied out over the plains, Nellie gaily waving her handerchief to those she left behind.

Ah, Nellie! Nellie! Little dream you of the snares that are laid to trip your pretty feet. Little know you of how your weaknesses have been studied and analyzed. Little suspect you that you may be used as a tool, and twisted around a strong woman's finger; and then thrust aside when your usefulness is over, and left bruised and bleeding in the dust. Poor, foolish, vain, weak Nellie!

CHAPTER VIII.

BLACKMAIL.

"COVILL," said the Judge, after agreeing to pay the detective one thousand dollars for a certain case, "it now becomes necessary for me to give you a further insight into the case that I have intrusted to you. In the first place, I wish to say that I fully appreciate your success thus far, and I assure you that you will never lose anything by your zeal in my behalf."

"I am certain of that, Judge," said Covill hastily, and in a manner conveying an apology for his recent greedy demand.

"And I wish to add," continued the Judge, bowing slightly for the compliment implied by Covill's words, "that I depend fully on your discreetness, your skill, and your faithfulness."

Covill was profuse in his thanks, and he mentally resolved to throw his whole soul into the work before him, and to never again distrust his employer's generosity and honor.

"Now, Covill, please give me your closest attention, and endeavor to fix in your memory every word that I am going to speak; for the matter is of some importance, and your best detective skill will be called into requisition.

"I am all attention, Judge."

The Judge remained buried in thought for some moments, and then he asked:

"Did the young man tell you whom he suspects of the crime?"

"Yes."

"What name did he mention?"

The detective glanced around furtively, assured himself that the doors were closed, and that no one could possibly be in hearing, and then leaned forward and whispered a name in the ear of the Judge, and then narrowly watched the effect.

"Did he say there were two?" asked the Judge, in profound astonishment.

"Yes."

"What makes him think that?"

"He refused to tell me."

"Ah!" exclaimed the Judge. "Well," he added, drawing a deep sigh, "the young man is in error; there was only one. But you must find out the reason for his idea. As soon as I heard that he was hunting for the treasure, I knew he had been communicated with, and it is to learn how much he knows and what he believes, that I sent you after him. Of course you secured the letter, did you not, Covill?"

"Yes; here it is," replied Covill, producing the letter, which the older man took and read with great interest.

"I am not sure, Covill," the Judge finally said, "but I am

strongly of the opinion that I know who wrote this letter. The work that lies before you now is to find that man without a moment's delay. Covill, the circumstances leading to the writing of this letter are so singular that they would seem to you the wildest romance. It was written for a far deeper purpose than that which it shows on its face. It may appear strange to you that I should know these things—indeed, it is more surmise than knowledge—but I am convinced that I understand the motive lying behind this letter. It is one of intense malignity and revenge; and young Graham has been cunningly selected as the tool for carrying a bad design into effect. I have no ill-feeling for the young man. I care nothing for him, and am indifferent about his concerns. I might even render him a service if it should come in my way; and certainly he will be incidentally benefited if we succeed in thwarting the designs that it is intended he shall carry out. You understand my position. I am considered a rich man, (though my wealth is greatly overrated) and as a capitalist, owning a great deal of land in the San Joaquin Valley; and as a man associated with many of the richest corporations in the State, as manager of some of the ramifications of their business, it hardly becomes me to be identified with a matter of such comparative insignificance as this matter seems to have. But on the other hand, as I have already said, there is a deeper meaning to this letter than at first appears. You know that there is in this State a loud-mouthed, dangerous element in the lower strata of society, and that it is composed of malcontents, discontented vagabonds, drunkards, and other idle and vicious persons. Because, by energy and superior judgment, some men, comparatively very few, have amassed fortunes, these low classes of society are jealous and envious. They howl about the aggressions of the rich, and shout themselves hoarse over the imaginary hardships that the powerful railroad and other monopolies impose. As you well know, we submit to persecutions without a murmur. These matters are notorious. The vicious persons—outlaws, thieves, foreigners, and discontented and mischievous persons from every quarter of the globe—these persons, composing the lower classes of society—the ignorant, coarse, and brutal—flock to California. This is the asylum for all the renegades of creation. As proof of the fact, note the opposition there is to wealth, and the power it wields. These men are organizing land leagues, secret societies, and a political party opposed to the so-called monopolies. Shrewd and unscrupulous rascals are really the leaders of this rebellious movement.

"Now this brings me to a direct consideration of the case in hand. These vicious and idle men concoct all kinds of schemes to annoy the capitalists and benefit themselves; and this mysterious letter emanates from such a source. It makes no difference to me whether or not the murder and robbery were committed. It is no concern of mine that the treasure was buried and then taken away. Covill, the writer of that letter *knew* the treasure had been removed. He was careful that it was not under Lone Tree when he wrote that letter. He reasoned in this manner: Young Graham will search for the treasure, and will not find it; he will feel great resentment toward some one, and will seek to find the treasure; then will be the time to direct his suspicions against some sympathizer with the railroad monopolists, and who is suspected by his neighbors of being in league against them—some powerful man who has incurred the enmity of others in Graham's neighborhood; and these will render him assistance in carrying out some desperate design against the person or persons on whom the suspicion will be cast. Do you follow me, Covill?"

The detective was completely absorbed in this recital, listening with the closest interest. He nodded in reply to the question.

"This will be all the more practicable, in view of the bitter feeling that now exists among the people of Mussel Slough—idle, vicious people, who have settled on land they know does not belong to them, and who seek to rob a useful corporation of it by exciting popular sympathy in their favor, as against the rich corporation that has done the only thing that could make that country desirable as a place of residence. You understand, now, that when these people of Mussel Slough are induced to believe that some such man as I mentioned just now has robbed this boy, they will be ready to rise up in arms and commit some terrible outrage. This is all clear to you, is it not?"

"Perfectly, sir."

"But that is not all. You see the importance of meeting this cunning movement with one equally as shrewd, and of nipping it in the bud before it can develop, and hence of finding the writer of this letter. As I said, however, that is not all. Who wrote this letter? I think I know. But another thing must be first considered. The name you mentioned to me just now has no significance for me. I know of no person bearing it. But don't you see that it would be the simplest matter in the world to find some man of that name who would swear that he was merely the tool of a rich man—I mean of a man who has become rich since the crime was committed?"

"I see."

"This would make the charge against the rich man the more plausible, as it would place him in the position of being exposed unwillingly by another man anxious to save his own neck."

Covill stared in open-mouthed admiration at the ingenuity of this logic.

"As I said, however, Covill," continued the capitalist, "the most interesting part of this matter remains to be told, and I will proceed at once, as my lawyer will soon return. The train of reasoning I have just followed up is based on something surer than mere surmises. As proof of it, I want you to read this letter, received by me several weeks ago:

"If you don't cease your persecutions, and allow me to earn an honest living, I shall tell something that I know."

The letter bore neither date, address, nor signature.

"Why," explained Covill, in great surprise, "this is the same handwriting as that of the letter to Graham!"

"Certainly."

"What does it mean?"

"Blackmail."

"But how?"

"Let me tell you something, Covill," said the capitalist, with an ugly glitter in his eyes: "that man is a fool who undertakes to run against the power of money. He finds himself encountering silent obstacles that he cannot understand. In California, a rich man is powerful, because as a rule his interests are common with those of other rich men. The community of great interests operates to the strengthening of the power of capital. This is a condition existing everywhere; but nowhere is it so great as in California. The reasons are quite plain, but it may be of service to you to know a few of them"; and he gave Covill a significant look. "The two great interests in this State are production and transportation. The great productions are those of agriculture and mining. Transportation is consolidated into one set of men, and the other interests are scattered among innumerable individuals, who are not organized. But many of these producers are extremely rich, and many of them, as individual persons, are strong enough to embarrass the operations of the transportation monopoly. The poorer producers are not. Hence it becomes necessary for certain favors to be shown the rich producers, and certain other favors are granted in return."

"In other words," interrupted Covill, with a sardonic grin, "it is a combination of the rich against the poor."

"That is the language of the sand-lot mob," said the capitalist, severely. Covill withered under the scornful look that accompanied this speech. "No, Covill; it is merely a measure for self-protection. Well, as I was going to say, this community of interests is strong enough to bring considerable discomfort to a man whose only means of earning a livelihood is that which capital offers to labor. Do you understand, Covill?"

"I think I do, sir; but it seems to me that any considerable exercise of such a power might eventually have the effect of accumulating a large number of men—large enough to do some mischief."

"Bah!" exclaimed the Judge, with disgust. "You are a fool, Covill. The remedy for such things is so simple that a child can understand it. A mere request addressed to the governor is all that would be necessary. He would call out the militia, and the militia would shoot down the fools. Why, Covill, I have even often wondered how the capitalists of this State can be so patient and forbearing as to permit abusive speeches and newspaper articles."

"I suppose the reason is," urged Covill, with much deference, "that these speeches and articles do no harm."

"That is it. Well, to continue the subject: not only is there a community of interests between capital and capital, but capital occupies a position in which it can extend minor favors to thousands and thousands of poor people, ambitious persons, politicians, and political leaders, and the many hundreds of thousands who are natural sycophants, and whom small favors will win. It is to such as these also that the influence of the corporations can extend in advancing or hindering the interests of others. Do you understand, Covill?"

Covill understood; and he at last also divined the true purport of this extended harangue, which was principally to make him appreciate his helplessness if he should in the least prove unfaithful to his trust. From that moment, Covill, being naturally weak, was a slave. The two men remained silent for some time, and then Covill asked:

"Do you know who wrote these two letters?"

"Yes: he is an idle, worthless fellow, whom I have shown more favors than one."

"Do you know where he is?"

"No; he became, like other men of his class, a malcontent, howling against rich men and the corporations. As a consequence, he lost employment, and disappeared. No doubt he is wandering over the country, trying to find people to listen to his incendiary tales. Why, Covill, you may judge the character of the man from the fact of his having committed a murder and a robbery, to say nothing of his having fooled this young man, and started him out to do mischief."

"You hinted at some singular circumstances. Have you told them all?"

"All that will be of any service to you; but as you are going to look for this man, and no doubt will find him, perhaps it will be better to inform you further. I know this man. He has been to me. He is a desperate, half-crazy man, and from his strange actions I judge that he must be guilty of some startling crime, and that it has been torturing him for many years. He magnifies his grievances; and there can no doubt that he is determined to leave nothing undone to bring trouble upon me."

The capitalist then furnished Covill with a minute description of the murderer; and then there followed a conversation, carried on a minute or two with bated breath. Covill turned pale and shuddered, and seemed undecided.

"I will shield you from all unpleasant consequences, Covill," said the elder man. "You know I am strong enough to do it. But at the same time it is necessary that you exercise the greatest care. Your disguise must be complete, and you must have no confederates or assistants. If you do the work carefully and thoroughly, I will give you five thousand dollars."

"I will do it," said Covill.

"As to Graham, you must take good care of him, and put him off from time to time; and in the mean time I will see that he is satisfied. Pretend to find a trace of the priest, who, I have no doubt, is a genuine priest; but you needn't waste any time looking for him. Covill," added the older man, after a pause, "the contingent reward that Graham offers you doesn't tempt you, does it? Even if you should get that money, Covill, it would never do you any good"; and the cold brown eyes of the old man looked the poor detective through and through. "It would never do you any good, Covill," he repeated.

Covill left, somewhat pale and nervous; and he was hardly out of sight when a lawyer entered from the studio, and said:

"Good morning, Judge Harriott."

CHAPTER IX.

COVILL'S ANNOUNCEMENT.

THE days dragged slowly by, and still John Graham's new ally was unable to report any definite progress. He complained of the heavy expense entailed by frequent trips to various parts of the country in following up blind trails that led nowhere. Graham did not become disheartened. It is true that the first glowing ardor he felt gradually cooled under these discouraging reports; and by degrees he brought himself to reflect calmly upon the magnitude of the enterprise. But his intention to search this mystery to its lowest depths and through its darkest ramifications abated not in the least, but rather came out in bolder relief as his excitement melted away. Such was his disposition. It was not by any sudden and violent change in his mind that this determination had framed itself. It had not burst upon him in a blaze of fire, the fierce raging of which would soon consume the fuel. It did not take shape when the mysterious letter was received; and it was only the discovery in the graveyard, and the calm reflection that followed it, that decided him upon the course he had adopted. It is true that this determination was more vivid and fierce while his excitement was high, but it was not more firm. He believed he was right, and that was sufficient for him. He believed that he and his had been wronged, and that was foundation enough for his resolution. He believed that it lay within the bounds of possibility to right these wrongs, and that was incentive enough to carry out the intentions of his dogged and inflexible will. If he was impatient before, he was calm and reasonable now.

It has been herein said concerning him, however, that there was much of stubbornness in his nature; but this would not unnecessarily obtrude itself, for it was counterbalanced by a considerable amount of caution. Still, it might assert itself under bitter and relentless persecution; for he chafed under restraint, scorned a power greater than that of his strong right arm, and when driven to an extremity would be capable of sacrificing his own interests, if by so doing he might overwhelm his enemy in the general ruin. In addition to this, it was not impossible for him to be thrown into a rage so terrible, so wild, so desperate, that nothing could stand before it—not even his own life. He felt to the full extent the sweet and wholesome restraints that his love for Nellie and his good old grandmother imposed; and the thought never entered his mind that consideration for them stood in his way in the least.

His slender stock of money was finally exhausted, and he saw that he must return to his home in the valley. He did not mentally complain at this. He charged nothing to fate. He did not curse his poverty and his feebleness. He bravely and without a murmur accepted whatever was, in store for him, and manfully believed that no blame should attach to anybody for the obstacles that lay in his way.

"Covill," he said one day, as that worthy person came to report. "I am going back home to-morrow. I can accomplish nothing here, and my money is exhausted. I shall leave everything to you, and I want you to report to me by letter every new aspect that the matter assumes."

It was a somewhat singular circumstance—although Graham, not being a close and quick observer, had failed to notice it—that whereas Covill had entered the room with his usual discouraged look, his face brightened when he learned Graham's intention, and he said briskly:

"Well, I think it's the best thing you can do; but before you start I want you to take something that may be of considerable comfort to you on the road."

"What is that?" asked Graham, interested at once.

"I have found a trail."

"Ah?"

"Yes."

"A hot one?"

"No; but a plain one."

"Good!"

"I knew I would in time."

"And I felt convinced of it."

"But it will take time to follow it up."

"That is no matter."

"Certainly not."

"We must be patient and watchful, Covill."

"That's the idea."

"Well, whose trail have you found?"

"The priest's."

"The priest's!"

"Yes."

"What is the clew?"

Covill pulled from his pocket a small note-book, and carefully turned the pages. Then he found what he wanted, cleared his throat with a manner conveying an idea of the satisfaction he felt with himself, and after glancing over some memoranda, said:

"On the 14th of December, 1876, Father Thomas, in charge of a small parish in this city, left home, saying he was in ill health and needed rest, and that he would take a short vacation, and would improve the time by visiting some former parishioners at Sacramento. But he had no intention of visiting Sacramento. There is no evidence that he ever bought a ticket. To make a long story short, I traced him to Lathrop, where the railroad turns to the south and passes through the San Joaquin Valley to Los Angeles and Fort Yuma. There I lost the trail."

"Is that all?"

"Not quite. After an absence of eight days, he returned. He then said that, after leaving San Francisco, he decided not to visit his old parishioners, and then he took a trip into the interior."

"Did he say where he went?"

"No. However, it will now be a simple matter to ascertain whether or not he is the man who dug up the Lone Tree treasure. All that I shall have to do is to make thorough inquiry in all the railroad towns of Fresno, Tulare, and Kern counties, for a priest who hired a horse and buggy on or about the 15th of December."

"That seems simple enough; but how will that lead you to the treasure?"

"Because it will lead me to the priest. It is necessary to be absolutely certain that Father Thomas is the man we want, before we can do anything with him."

Graham shook his head dubiously. He had an idea of his own.

"I think there is a better plan than that, Covill."

"What is it?"

"I will go directly to the priest, surprise him with the charge, and demand the money or his life.

Covill turned slightly pale.

"Suppose he refuses to divulge the secret?"

"I will compel him to."

"But he would cry out and raise the alarm."

"You are wrong. He would not cry out." This was said with a certain gloomy fierceness.

"How would you prevent it?"

"You shall see."

"He may be stronger than you."

"No thief is a good fighter."

"Besides," urged Covill, whose wits had been very busy during this conversation, "you can hardly have the pleasure of an interview with this reverend gentleman."

"Why?"

"For the simple reason that on Christmas day, which was

two days after his return, he conducted high mass in the morning, and then left the city."

"What!"

"He has gone."

Graham, who had risen, now sat down, almost overwhelmed by this new misfortune.

"Why didn't you tell me that at first?" he demanded severely.

"You didn't give me a chance before you announced your determination to pay him a visit; and then I thought I would wait and find out what you intended to do."

"Then you trifled with me, Covill!" exclaimed Graham, angrily, and with a look in his eyes that meant mischief. "Be careful how you try that in future."

Covill feared the young man heartily, and often wished that he had never seen Graham. It may be said in Covill's favor, that the time had been when he was not a bad man at heart. His downfall dated from the time when he was picked up, a hungry and homeless emigrant from the East, by certain men who saw in his poverty and need an opportunity to make him a faithful and useful tool, by giving him employment and placing him under obligations. He had been gradually and insensibly drawn into the performance of a kind of unmanly and secret surveillance over persons in the employment of one of the great railroad companies; and finally he had been led into nefarious detective work, such as that in which he was engaged for the man called Judge Harriott.

In this connection a curious phase of human nature.

under the operation of the power that the seemingly invincible corporations—the greater ones—of California wield, presents itself, and Covill is a fair illustration. It is based on the peculiar system of rewards and inducements that are tacitly understood between employer and servant, as being held out to the latter for fidelity in the discharge of his duties. This silently accepted contract is that the servant is recognized as being under the influence of no obligations that do not directly concern the interests of his employer. The more faithful he is to the charge thus imposed and accepted, the more sure will be his promotion, and the more rapid will be the advancement of his own private interests, and the greater becomes his reflected influence and power. Let him raise a finger against his employer's benefit, even if it be in the protection of some private right, or the assertion of independent manhood and citizenship, and he had as well go and hang himself. He is made not only a slave, but a coward also.

Covill found himself in such a predicament.

"But," he would gravely moralize, "they stand by a fellow, and pay him handsomely."

Covill announced to Graham strong hope of finding the priest, but declared that his first duty was to become assured of the identity; and on the following day Graham mounted his horse and rode away.

CHAPTER X.

NEW DEVELOPMENTS.

GRAHAM was not too deeply absorbed in his plans to overlook a change that had taken place since he had left his quiet home in the valley. They were all very glad to see him, to be sure. The good old grandmother clung to his neck, and covered his face with kisses.

And Nellie? She, too, was glad, but not in the old way. She had returned from that enchanting trip to the lake, which had afforded her such a round of pleasure and excitement as she had longed for during her whole life. In that short time she had learned more of the world than ordinary girls would have learned in a life-time. Her quick and sharp perception had put her in possession of seemingly an inexhaustible store of information concerning the ways of people of the world. Those with whom she had associated were persons of wide information, and belonged to that social class that is one degree below the highest, and that observes conventionalities more for the sake of the benefit and pleasure it derives from them than for the sake of being formal. In what is termed the highest social circle individuality is impossible, because it is an infringement of rules. It is purely mechanical and automatic. It can talk of books, music, and painting; but it cannot produce them, because it dare not, even if by some mischance it had proper training and sufficient mental development. With Nellie's new friends it was different. They were bold enough to enjoy life. They were daring enough to assert that there are beautiful and grand things in nature. Even if God does work and they did not, they did not feel themselves superior to Him. They would even have felt themselves moved by curiosity to pay a visit of inspection to the humble Nazarene, if He should appear in the world. They were not, as are their social superiors, vapid, empty, and weak. They laughed heartily when amused. They cried out when in pain. They walked, if riding was less convenient. They enjoyed life, and made the most of it; and such were natures with which Nellie's could affiliate. She learned a thousand pretty little tricks from Alice—perfectly natural with Alice, by reason of habits hastened by a life-time of practice, but new to Nellie. The country girl was changed; still she was too sensible to make herself appear silly in the eyes of her plain friends, although she had a very charming way of pretending to be unconscious of many slyly taken little departures from habits that she had known before.

It is not matter of surprise that noble, sturdy, big-hearted John, whom she had always regarded as a latent hero, appeared smaller in her eyes than formerly. He was not witty and wise, as were the men with whom she had recently associated. His hair was not trimmed in conventional style. His mustache was ragged and neglected. His hands were not soft and white. His clothes, bought ready-made at the village, were painfully unfashionable, and did not fit him well. His cravat was obsolete and absolutely ugly. His shoes were coarse, heavy, and rough. His hat presented a painful contrast to the natty ones of her friends from the city. Besides all that, he did not eat soup from the side of his spoon, and permitted the forefinger of his right hand to extend too far on the blade of his knife while eating. He did not think of the performance of a thousand of those trifling and delicate attentions that a well-bred man shows a woman. He was very dull and stupid. He had never heard an opera nor seen a drama. It never occurred to him to ascertain the authorship of some book that pleased him, for he was in that crude condition when effects are seen and causes overlooked.

But Nellie knew (as she was in many respects a sensible girl) that not one of her new male friends could ride as well as John; that none were as strong and active as he; that none could endure such hardships and brave such perils as he could. But it was not in Nellie's nature (and therefore she should not be blamed for it) to go deeper than this, and place John's grander manhood on a higher pedestal in her mind than that occupied by the polished and shallower men she had come to know.

John did not see and understand all these things, although he felt that a change had taken place in Nellie. It is true that she did not seem to love him less; but there was now a certain superiority in her manner toward him, that he felt rather than saw. If he had known more of the world and human nature, and had been quicker of perception and understanding, and had possessed more natural tactics, he could have seen, analyzed, and checked the dangerous change that had taken place in the mind rather than the heart of the girl he loved and hoped to make his wife. If he had been such a man, he could have torn the painted mask from the faces of his natural inferiors, and exposed to her view the shallowness that lay concealed underneath.

But even if he could have done all this it might not have availed to quiet the storm of unrest and dissatisfaction that had arisen in Nellie's breast; for it was to such a one as she that the serpent offered the apple in the Garden of Eden— a light heart, and yet a loving and clinging one withal; a longing for that which effort may obtain; a soul that must have a brighter and more glittering idol than one bringing only rest and peace and happiness.

She was not less happy and cheerful than before, even though she knew her own plain clothing was inadequate for all the purposes for which a woman's clothing is intended; even though the manners of those about her were coarse and uncouth. The dainty and precise old grandmother, a sworn enemy of dirt and disorder, no longer held sway over Nellie as an autocrat of punctiliousness and good taste.

But for all that, she was none the less bright and cheerful; and the reason of this lies in the fact that she hoped for a brighter day, believing that her influence over John would be sufficient as a means for her appearing, sooner or later, in that sphere that she felt she was made to adorn. Poor, foolish Nellie!

Well, the grandmother and John returned to their home, and the old quiet order of things was apparently restored. The sweet old lady was glad that John never spoke of the missing treasure. In the bottom of her heart—much as she wished for his sake that he might be rich and prosperous—she humbly thanked God that they were poor, as thereby her boy was spared to her yet a while longer. He was all she had, and all she prayed for, and all she loved, and all the light and life she had in the world, and all that kept her patient soul and her withered old body together. She almost hoped that he had abandoned the undertaking, and she carefully refrained from mentioning it. He went about his duties as usual. A casual observer would have noticed no change in him.

He had not abandoned his resolution; but it is true that at times he analyzed his own motives with no lenient scrutiny. At times he would ask himself:

"Is my motive a good one? Is it not true that my desire to secure the fortune is really the only motive that actuates me? Is it not possible that I am given over to avarice? The murderer has made all the atonement in his power. It would not have come too late if his wishes and intentions had resulted as he wanted them to. Would it be fair and manly to hunt him down? Let me look this matter squarely in the face. Is it seemly that I should suddenly develop a determination to avenge my father's murder at this late day, in view of my ability to have formed such a resolution some years ago? I must admit to myself that a desire to see justice dealt out is not at the bottom of my motives. I must confess the truth, and admit that it is the money I want. Why should I not want it? It is mine. Did I earn it? If not, is it mine? It was my father's. I inherit all that was my father's, including the wrong that was done. I inherit his money, and it is mine. It cannot belong to the man who stole it: then to whom can it belong? To none but me. Am I avaricious in claiming my own? Surely not. Let me, then, fairly understand myself. It is the money I should look for, and I will look for it. Not only my father was robbed, but I also. Therefore I also have been subjected to outrage. If my father had not been killed and robbed, I would have that money to-day. Then certainly I have been robbed, just as surely as if I had first come into the possession of the money before the robbery was committed. Therefore I must not submit like a hound. I must show my manhood and demand my rights. But the robber has, so far as good intention goes, restored the money to me. Can I punish him? No; but I must have the money. He has made atonement, and I accept his act as such. I forgive him the robbery, and hope that God can pardon the murder. But I have been robbed a second time, and this time by a priest! Very well; the priest must beware. I will regard him as a highwayman, and will hunt him as such, and will treat him as such when I find him. He will be the object of my search. I will find him. I will punish him. I will have my money."

Occasionally he received letters from Covill, which were

indefinite and unsatisfactory, although they were hopeful. Graham remained quiet and patient, believing that the money, being in the hands of a priest, was in no great danger of being squandered. He would give Covill ample opportunity to do whatever he could do. There would be time to take other steps when Covill failed.

In the mean time, Nellie had not been neglected by Mrs. Harriott, who wrote kind letters to the county girl, and sent her a book now and then, which Nellie eagerly read.

One fine day Nellie's heart violently bounded with joy when she received an urgent invitation to visit Mrs. Harriott, who had been so considerate as to inclose a railroad ticket. Now did Nellie's cheeks glow, and now did her bright eyes become brighter still, and now was she triumphant. "Do not be uneasy concerning your wardrobe," the letter said; "we shall arrange that all when you come. I need you now, because in a few days Alice will formally enter the world. I want you to be with her, for you have a clear head and a good heart, and you can assist her a great deal. I shall look for you very soon. Do not disappoint us. Of course Alice joins me in this invitation, and Judge Harriott sends you his kindest regards, and hopes you will come."

Was there ever a grander triumph? Was not Heaven kind to grant her this great boon—the one that her heart yearned for more than all else? The folks at home were proud of the honors showered upon Nellie; and even John, dearly as he loved the girl, told her it would be good for her to go, and that for such a reason he would cheerfully give her up for a time. Nellie's preparations were soon completed; and before she had fully come to realize the sweetness and brightness of the glorious light that had burst upon her life, the cars were bearing her rapidly to San Francisco. Poor, light-hearted Nellie!

She must have received many flattering attentions at San Francisco, for her letters were encyclopedias of news and gossip. Mrs. Harriott had given her fine clothes, and a piece of jewelry now and then; and beyond a doubt, Nellie was admired, and had at last come to enjoy a realization of her fondest dreams.

John was pleased that Nellie was happy.

One day Nellie wrote him that he could secure a position in the service of the railroad company, and urged him to accept it. She explained that she had talked so much about him to her new friends, that they had become interested in him, and wished to do something for him. "To be sure," said Nellie's letter, "the position is not a high one; but you would soon be promoted, until finally you would come to occupy one of the highest positions with the company. The work will not require your absence all the time from home; but you could be with us two or three days every week." The position was that of a brakeman for a freight train—a humble position, and one entailing very hard work; but it would throw him more upon the world, and would give him a far better opportunity for carrying out his plans than he possessed. Nevertheless, it was a subject deserving serious consideration, for reasons that will presently appear. Under other circumstances, Graham would not have considered it a matter of extraordinary importance; but there were some things to be taken into consideration, which John, careful and farseeing, did not lose sight of. The thought had never occurred to him that Nellie had been drawn into a plot against him; but he was shrewd enough to see some of the dangers that lay ahead of him. He did not fear them, and considered only the proposition whether or not it would be possible to turn these dangers to account.

Although Graham was ignorant in experience of the world, he had very good general information through reading; and he was acquainted with many of the particulars of a distressing condition of affairs that had arisen in his own section of country, and that affected him to no trifling extent. Matters were taking a serious turn in affairs that concerned him deeply, as well as they did many others who were similarly situated. Violent disturbances were about to occur, and their magnitude impressed him. They were apart from the work he had in hand, but he saw that they would affect his plans. It is no wonder that he seriously considered all the bearings these new developments would have on his plans and his prospects, and that he reflected carefully on the position he would occupy as a servant of the railroad company. He did not suspect any trap that was laid for him, and did not dream of any plans, to which Nellie had become a party, for overreaching him and crippling his operations. He decided to wait a while.

CHAPTER XI

A TRAGEDY ON THE PLAINS.

MEANWHILE, Covill had not been idle. In place of courage, which he did not possess to a remarkable degree, he had energy and perseverance. Moreover, he was very shrewd, and was by nature fitted to be a successful detective; and he was animated by that zeal which is seen in all the servants, from the highest to the lowest, of those great corporations of California that take possession of a man's conscience as well as his hands; that fasten on him, sucking his manhood dry; that cling to him with the tenacity of a nightmare which cannot be shaken off, and from which there is no waking. In whose service did he show this zeal? In Graham's? Surely not! Graham was poor, and consequently weak. Being unable to grind down the poverty of others to a deeper poverty still; to harass and exterminate those who opposed him; to put a gag of gold in the mouths of men who might otherwise publish to an ignorant and careless world horrible truths of injustice and oppression; to buy legislators like sheep, and herd them like cattle; to hold a high hand over the welfare and destiny of hundreds of thousands of human beings created in the image of God; to hire judges and bribe juries; to send a traitor wherever possible into every community, and put one down at every fireside to set man against man, and thus break the strength of the whole;—being unable to do all this, or any part of it, and being too grand and honest and charitable and human to do it had he the power, he was not the one who first claimed Covill's attention. The tentacles of the octopus were around Covill's soul as well as his arms. As he was, he was merely a part —a very small part—of the great weight that has been chained to the necks of the people of this grand country of gold and wheat and fruit and wine. He did his work faithfully, as did all the others with whom and for whom he worked. He was one of the cogs in this great wheel that grinds men down to desperation, and that has at last driven them to the wall; where, let it be hoped by every man whose mind has not been clouded nor soul corrupted, the wounded bear may show his teeth, and like the hounded grizzly of the Sierra, tear with claw and rend with teeth whatever seeks its death.

Covill had found a trail, but not that of the priest. He cared nothing for the priest. His conscience felt no sting that he had fooled and cheated Graham with the story of Father Thomas, who, so far as Covill knew, had never been in existence. The trail that he had found was that of the man who had written the letter that told of the Lone Tree treasure. This is the manner in which he made that important discovery: Armed with the minute description that

Judge Harriott had furnished, he had put himself in communication with every leading officer of the constabulary in that stretch of country embracing and immediately surrounding the valley of the Sacramento, and his efforts were soon rewarded by a response that announced the discovery of the man. Covill had not far to go to find him, for the mysterious man, when discovered, was begging a living among the comfortable homes that nestle cozily in the foothills east of Berkeley and Temescal.

Covill found him easily, and paid a handsome reward to the officer who had rendered such valuable service. And the fact may here be noted that this was not the first time that inferior officers of local civil government (it is a foregone conclusion that superior civil officers have been generally the more useful in furthering the schemes of the powerful corporations)—this was not the first time that an inferior officer had exhibited a collateral zeal for a power that has become greater than that mythical thing which, by ignorant persons, is sometimes called a government by the people. People! Why, there are no people in California! There are no farmers, no miners, no merchants, no manufacturers, no wine-makers! If there are, where are they? Search narrowly for them. Visit the State courts and the Federal courts. Look on and under the cushioned seats in the Capitol building. Are they there? Surely not! Now and then one of the people is found raising his voice above the sound of the clink of gold; but he had as well be, for all that he can do without the help of others, a quiet sleeper under the shadow of Lone Mountain, or a homeless spirit in the other world.

Having found his man, Covill shadowed him. He was an old man—nearly sixty years old. He belonged to that great army of beggars known as "tramps"—wanderers from house to house: who may be worthy objects of charity, but who generally are able-bodied men, finding it easier to gain a livelihood by imposing on the credulity of tender-hearted people than by earning an honest and manly living; men who invest in whisky all the money that misplaced benevolence gives them, and the half of whose time is passed in sleeping off, in some fence corner or deserted field, the effects of intoxication; petty thieves, who rob hen-roosts and devastate potato patches: a worthless, lazy lot altogether, undeserving of a morsel to eat; yet among whom there may now and then be one in dire need of whatever may keep soul and body together, that he may not die on the highway of hunger. These are very rare, but sometimes they are found. Sometimes they, having angered a rich and powerful corporation, find themselves stranded in the search for honest employment, and yet have not the courage and independence to cross the Rocky Mountains, and commence the battle beyond the reach of the terrible tentacles of the devil-fish.

Harris (for this was the name by which he was known) was not withheld by lack of courage for seeking other parts of the country. He had a mission to fill—an atonement to make. The crime of eighteen years ago had haunted him during all those dreary years—years crowded with the bitter pangs of conscience—with poverty and hunger and persecution, when he would have tried to become a better man. By some he was called an incendiary—which in California has come to mean a man who dares speak out against the oppressions that are weighing the people to the earth. He gathered crowds together, and told of his wrongs, and the wrongs of hundreds and thousands of others who had not yet been brought by persecution to the depth in which he groveled. For this, and for the outspoken honesty of his utterances, he was a marked man, and could easily be found. Petty civil officers, anxious to obey the behests of a lordly power greater than the shadowy democracy of the people's power, and fawning at the feet of that corrupted life-center that sends poisoned blood through every artery of the State's body, were on the alert for such as Harris. It was to them small matter that he had killed a man, and thereby offended the "peace and dignity of the people of California"; but it was important that, weak as he was, he had trodden on the corns of money. There is greater reward in store for those who serve the corporations than there is for those who carry out the wishes of that nominal but feeble and imbecile master called the law—a king who has been stripped of his crown and his purple robe, and whose scepter is gone.

It was for such reasons that Covill found his man so readily; and Covill had known, and so had Judge Harriott, that the search need not be long and tedious. The strongest master is first obeyed.

Covill shadowed his man; but Covill was no longer the Covill whose face was familiar to and who was so much dreaded by some men who had already been crushed under the Juggernaut wheel of the golden idol—men whom he had watched and hounded for petty shortcomings, or men who had dared vote in an election contrary to the commands of their master. Covill's disguise was complete. He had shaved his mustache, and had allowed a short stubble to grow all over his face. He had become a "tramp," and he wore ragged clothes and dusty shoes.

He fell in with Harris, and bore him company. He begged with Harris from door to door. He slept with Harris in abandoned hay-ricks. He drank with Harris from streams and ditches, and ate with Harris the crusts that were given them, and traveled with Harris day and night. In a burst of confidence he told Harris of imaginary crimes committed, which were not half so cowardly as the one he contemplated—and cowardice is at the bottom of every wrong of omission or of commission that is done. He hoped that Harris would reciprocate with similar confidences, but Harris was discreetly still. Moreover, any confessions by Harris were unnecessary, as Covill became assured beyond the possibility of error that Harris was the man he sought. Why did he not deliver Harris up to the authorities or to Judge Harriott? The reason will soon appear.

Harris was weary and disturbed. His sleep was broken by incoherent utterings and frequent nightmares. His right leg, on which he limped slightly, and which he said he had broken when he was a boy, frequently ached under the fatigue of a day's long wanderings, and he complained of it. At other times he would say that he wished he was dead; but that he had one duty to perform in life; that already he had made one attempt, but it had failed, he feared; and that he would go in person and do that which he feared a letter he had written had failed to do.

He liked Covill, and gladly accepted the companionship that Covill offered. He was friendless and lonely, and he hungered for a word of sympathy and kindness, and Covill furnished these in abundance. They cost Covill nothing; and Covill had by habit become a sycophant and a flatterer. He cheered the homeless old man, and brought some companionship and comfort into his life.

Led by Harris, the two men pushed their way slowly southward, until one day they found themselves on the bank of the San Joaquin River. The river was full of water from the melting snows of the Sierra, and it was with some difficulty that they finally succeeded in discovering a shelf in the wall of the western bank, that they might be protected from the cold night wind that came from the north. Having found such a spot—and Harris, if he had had any suspicions, might have noticed that it was Covill's desire to be as far from any road as possible—they camped. It was in the forenoon, and they decided to sleep that night in the place they had selected.

If Harris had been suspicious, he might have noticed that Covill did not relish the homely meal they prepared with a fire made of drift-wood. He might also have seen that, as the time passed slowly by, Covill became restless and uneasy. He could not sit still, and he walked incessantly back and forth on the narrow shelf, now and then throwing a pebble into the river. But Harris, worn, old, and weighted down by something that oppressed his mind, noticed none of these things, or, if he did, paid no attention to them. The crime that haunted him had been committed too long ago for him to fear sudden danger; and the surreptitious look of suspicion that murderers are apt frequently to throw around had long ago disappeared. Furthermore, Harris was not naturally suspicious, and he did not dream of the presence of danger. Yet danger there was—dark and bloody danger—cold, cruel, and murderous danger, that followed his every motion, and that awaited only a good opportunity to perform its deadly work.

Harris found a sunny spot on the grass-grown shelf, and stretched himself to sleep. In a few minutes he was slumbering soundly, and Covill's time had come.

He had been furtively watching the old man, and when he saw by the heavy, regular breathing of his victim that he was asleep, Covill drew a deep breath, and his heart bounded wildly with terrible excitement. Then he arose and stretched himself, and mincingly approached the sleeping man. They were below the level of the plains, and were invisible from any point of the surrounding country, and were a long distance from any human habitation; but to assure himself again of these facts, Covill ascended to the top of the bank and looked around. No living thing was visible, except here and there a gopher or an owl.

Covill silently descended to the niche on which they had encamped. Harris still slept heavily, and but for the regular heaving of his breast in slumber he might have been taken for a dead man. He lay on his back, with his arms extended on the ground, his legs apart, and his face shaded by his ragged old hat. Covill thanked his good fortune that the face of his victim was concealed.

Covill pulled from a sheath concealed in his clothing a long, bright, sharp hunting-knife—the most deadly weapon that ever entered the vitals of a man. He held it in such a manner that his arm concealed the blade, and then stealthily approached the sleeping man.

The terrible excitement of the moment unnerved Covill. A cold perspiration broke out on his face. His teeth chattered as though he had ague. He was cold to the marrow, and his knees trembled under his weight. At the last moment his heart failed, and he precipitately retreated, and again clambered to the level of the plains. Then he sat down, weak and almost fainting, and tried to collect his thoughts, and nerve himself for the bloody work in hand. He looked like a man who was hunted for his life.

A novel idea occurred to him. Surrounding him was a quantity of drift-wood that some heavy flood had brought down from the mountains and lodged upon the bank. Among these pieces of wood was a large, heavy log, that lay very near the brink of the bluff. If that log should be rolled down upon the sleeping man below, it would crush out his life before he could realize his situation. Covill breathed a deep sigh of relief as this simpler plan presented itself. He looked over the bluff, and saw Harris still quietly sleeping, and knew that the log, if rolled over the bank, would fall directly upon the sleeper. He looked around. Still no one was in sight.

Then he sought and found a strong piece of wood, that he could use as a lever with which to move the log.

Having found it, he proceeded silently to work. He secured a thick piece of wood that served for a fulcrum, and then he tried his lever. It was strong, sure, and unyielding. He inserted one end under the middle of the log, placed the fulcrum in position, and gradually put his weight on the lever. The log moved a few inches. With his foot he pushed the fulcrum forward, and again threw his weight on the lever. The log rolled silently. One more turn would hurl it full upon the prostrate form of the sleeper.

Covill drew a deep breath as he realized that in two or three more seconds his work would be finished. Again he placed the fulcrum and lever in position, peered over the bank to see if Harris still slept, and then held his breath and ground his teeth as he gave the lever another pull.

The heavy log reached the brink, toppled a moment, and then fell with a heavy crash.

A short, sharp, smothered scream of agony was all that Covill heard, and then all was still and silent; and, not daring to look down on the ghastly scene that his imagination depicted, he bounded away and over the plains like a frightened deer, heading for the Coast Range; never suspecting that his victim might be only half killed, nor that he was caught as in a vise, to await a death more horrible and torturing than any that Covill's ingenuity could have conceived.

CHAPTER XII.

THE "SAND-LAPPERS."

THE considerations that deterred Graham from immediately accepting the situation offered him through Nellie were indeed of a grave character, deserving careful thought. They pointed to complications that would sooner or later, if the natural progress of human events should take the course that seemed inevitable, involve him in a catastrophe of which he would not be the only victim.

The change that had taken place in his disposition caused no little concern on the part of those who were parties to some of the impositions. It was reflected that he evinced in one direction a disposition that would be dangerous in another. He was soon to be assailed by perils independent of those growing out of his search for the stolen treasure, yet perils that would affect that search vitally. In order to understand these brewing difficulties and their subsequent applications to Graham's affairs, it will be necessary to take a cursory glance at a matter that had already become a part of the history of the county and the State, and that was destined to lead to red-handed violence.

Graham, in company with many other persons, and notably with the majority of those who had made their homes in the Mussel Slough country, had settled upon land claimed by the railroad company, or for which the railroad company had been for some time awaiting patents from the United States, the company having promised these settlers deeds when the patents should be received.

This Mussel Slough country has, by reason of the troubles that have grown out of its settlement and occupation, become the most noted section of California. It stretches for several miles north and north-east of Tulare Lake, and embraces parts of Tulare and Fresno counties, but lies principally in the former. It takes its name from a slough that makes out from the lake. It produces, by reason of the vast amount of work done by the settlers in improving it, the finest crops of grain and fruit in the State, and its climate is more inviting than that of any other portion of the great stretch of country lying between the Coast Range and the Sierra Nevada Mountains.

This much having been said, the purpose of an important visit that Graham received will soon be apparent. His exploit at Lone Tree had been noised abroad, and had brought him considerable notoriety, and great was the popular interest taken in his affairs; and attention had been drawn more especially to strange stories—nearly all of them unfounded in fact—that had been circulated concerning him and his movements, to such an extent that people had come to look upon him as a young man possessing unusual nerve and energy. Prior to that time he was almost unknown in the county, and had been regarded as simply one of the many unfortunate persons who had fallen into the clutches of a powerful monopoly. Be it said, in explanation, that at the time of the opening of this story he had lived but a short time upon the new home that he had bought from the railroad company.

His name had become familiar to all, and the eyes of the troubled people of Mussel Slough were turned toward him hopefully, as to a man whose clear head could assist them in the difficulties that had overtaken them.

His visitor was a man of middle age, well bred, and a farmer. His name was Newton. Graham welcomed him; and after a desultory conversation, Newton asked:

"Have you seen a man who is said to be at work in Mussel Slough affixing prices to these so-called railroad lands that we settled upon?"

Graham had not seen him.

"Well," continued Newton, "there is no doubt that there is a man here on such a mission; and as you are in a position similar to that of us who settled on these lands, I thought I would come to put you on your guard, and to ask you to go to Hanford with me to-day to attend a meeting of the settlers."

"How long has this man been here?"

"They say he has been seen for some time, but his real mission wasn't suspected until recently."

"I will go," said Graham.

They started without delay for Hanford; but they had not proceeded far when they overtook a horseman. This man was a stranger, and his appearance at such a time naturally aroused the curiosity of Newton and Graham.

"Good morning, sir," said Newton.

"Good morning," greeted he them in return. "I am taking a look at the country," he added pleasantly. "I understand that some of these lands will soon be offered for sale, and I came to inspect them."

A quick look of intelligence passed between Graham and his companion.

"Then you are not a 'sand-lapper,'" said Newton, quietly.

"A what?" asked the stranger, in surprise.

"A 'sand-lapper.'"

"And what in the world is a 'sand-lapper'?"

"You are evidently a stranger in this part of the country," answered Newton, "or you would know the meaning of the term."

"It is a very strange expression, and I should like to know the meaning of it."

"The term," said Newton, "is one of derision that the cattle lords applied to the first settlers on these sandy plains, on account of the eagerness displayed by the settlers in taking up the seemingly barren lands. The cattle men said that if the settlers lived at all they must eat sand."

"So far as I am able to judge," said the stranger, with a smile, "the settlers seem to thrive exceedingly well on the diet."

"It is because they succeeded in getting from the sand wheat, fruit, and alfalfa."

"But why," persisted the stranger, as the three traveled

along together, "did the cattle men, as you call them, think the settlers would have to eat sand? Surely, I never saw a more glorious country than this. Look at that wheat field there. Was there ever a grander sight?"

"Well," said Newton, "this country was at one time called sterile; and such a desolate appearance did it have, that the cattle men said they would not pay fifty cents an acre for it. Now, you see, it is one vast wheat field."

And indeed the prospect was glorious. None who have been denied the pleasure of visiting Mussel Slough in the spring-time can form any idea of the enchanting scene that the entire face of the country presents. Here is a broad stretch of wheat; and a little farther on one finds a patch of alfalfa—a darker and richer green; and a little farther on appears an orchard in full bloom.

"Before I give you the interesting piece of history that explains this matter," said Newton, "may I ask you how you learned that these lands are for sale, and who offers them?"

"A friend wrote to me," replied the man, without hesitation. "I have very little information on the subject, and would be glad to have more. As I understand it—though doubtless you are better informed than I—every odd section of this land is owned by the railroad company, which has been greatly annoyed by squatters who have taken possession of the land."

"Ah, they have poisoned you too!" said Newton, bitterly "The 'squatters,' sir," he added with some severity, "are men who are betrayed; who have earned what they have by privations too bitter for you to even comprehend them; who are acting honestly and in good faith; and who are struggling to retain their own from the grasp of a robber."

The stranger gazed at Newton in astonishment.

"And it is such men as you," continued Newton, "who are sent here to buy from under us the land we have earned at the price of hunger and indescribable sufferings. I am one of those terrible 'sand-lappers.'"

The stranger was aghast with amazement at these assertions and at Newton's warmth.

"I assure you," he said, "that I will not be a party to any wrong. Let us understand that at once. And now I should like to hear the history of this whole matter."

Newton made no reply for some time, as the men rode leisurely along; and finally he said:

"Well, I see that you have been imposed upon, and that you are ready to listen to reason. It would take too long to go into full details, and I can merely glance at the more important particulars. In the first place, no reasonable man having any knowledge of the facts believes that the railroad company owns these lands."

"What!" exclaimed the stranger. "I understand the Government has issued patents to the lands."

"Yes; but the conditions to be fulfilled by the company never were complied with, and there is room for grave suspicion as to how the patents were obtained."

"What were those conditions?"

"Briefly stated, they were these: The company was to secure the patents upon the completion of every twenty-five consecutive miles of the road running westward from Goshen, through the heart of Mussel Slough, through the Coast Range to the Santa Clara Valley. These patents were issued after only twenty of the required twenty-five miles were completed; and then the company, having secured the lands, violated the contract with the Government by refusing to make the road a through line. Besides all that, the twenty miles were not constructed within the time required by the Act of Congress."

"Then why were the patents issued?"

"Why!" exclaimed Newton with great bitterness; "why is it that land is given in unlimited quantities to rich men and corporations, while we poor devils have to pay for it and live on it? Why is it that money controls our Congress, and carries corruption into every branch of the Government—and always in favor of the rich and at the expense of the poor? But let us assume that the company legally holds the lands, and we can't deny that it has broken faith with us, and that it now undoubtedly has on foot the most stupendous scheme of blackmailing that was ever attempted in this country."

"That is a strong charge. What do you mean?"

"It invited settlers to come upon these lands, offering to give them preference over any others when patents should be received, and offering the lands at two dollars to five dollars an acre, and declaring that the settlers would not be charged for any improvements they might make when the time should come for paying for the lands."

"That was fair," said the stranger.

"Yes; but I hear that a man has just arrived in this section to place prices on the lands for the railroad company, and he says that he is instructed to include in the rates the added value that this great system of irrigating ditches has given this country."

"Surely no men, and especially rich men, could be guilty of so great a wrong!"

"Ah, you don't know these men! And the world will never know the terrible hardships that we of Mussel Slough underwent on the strength of the promises held out to us."

"What kind of hardships?"

Newton looked around, and saw a comfortable cottage to the right.

"Let us take the case of the people living in that house," he said. "It is a history common to nearly all of us. In 1870 this family moved to Mussel Slough. At that time the whole country was covered with live stock. It was the range of the cattle men, who held possession of these vast plains. The first efforts of this family were in the direction of improvements, and they planted an orchard on a piece of ground near the slough, hoping there would be sufficient water for the growth of the trees."

"But it seems that anything can grow here," interposed the stranger.

"That has been accomplished by irrigation," said Newton. "At that time Mussel Slough was an arid, sandy desert, yielding only a meager supply of grass for the herds of horses, cattle, sheep, and hogs that covered the plains. Well, the stock devoured the fruit trees and vines. The stock men looked upon the settlers as intruders, and did everything possible to discourage them and drive them away. I arrived here about that time, and lived near this family. We traveled in a wagon a hundred miles and back for seed-wheat, paying a heavy price. We planted it, and had to dig a deep, broad ditch to protect our grain from the stock, and this required incalculably hard work. Then came the blackbirds and crows, which picked up the grain. Mind you, this is not merely an individual experience. There were hundreds of us who underwent these trials. That year we cut the wheat for hay; and by the time it was cut and taken care of the overflowed lands around the lake were drying; and the settlers, many of them living several miles away, secured little patches of this damp ground, and planted corn. I and the family we have just passed were of the number. Well, sir, we had to actually sleep beside our corn to keep away the horses and cattle."

"That was a hardship indeed."

"But a very trifling one in comparison with others," said Newton, smiling. "With all our work, day and night, the stock would have well-beaten tracks through the fields. We hauled away the corn stalks to feed to our horses; and when we took them home we had to sleep on them to keep away the stock that covered the plains; and even then the hungry cattle would eat over our heads, while we slept from exhaustion. The no-fence law, which had the effect of requiring the stock men to keep their cattle off the farms, was a godsend to the settlers, as the high price of lumber rendered fencing an impossibility. The people were glad to get even cheap, thin boards, split by hand, with which to build their cabins, some of which was made of the tules that grow on the lake shore."

"That is almost incredible!"

"But none the less true; and you have not heard the worst yet. These miserable hovels offered poor protection against the terrible sand-storms that swept the plains."

"Did it not discourage you?"

"Some were so discouraged that they abandoned their homes and left for better parts. Those who remained left the lake; and as there was a little rain that year we decided to plant a crop on the land we had originally settled. We were kept busy driving off the stock. Two daughters in the family I mentioned just now were in the saddle from morning till night for that purpose; and they would drive a band of horses to the owner, in Fresno County, only to find them again in the grain when they returned. I have known those brave girls to become so discouraged that they would go into their poor house and sit down and cry; and then get heart again, and return to the endless task. Our crop was not more than a foot high when the drouth came and killed it. The ditches that we now have render a drouth comparatively harmless. We all turned out and pulled up our grain by the roots, in order to not lose an inch of the stalks by cutting them, and we stacked it for our horses. All that we had to eat was the seed that had cost us so much. The stock men took hope, and believed we would be driven out by starvation. Provisions were so expensive that we could not afford to buy any. The stock men would not even sell us meat. We found some beans, and killed wild hogs in the tules. This flesh tasted so strong of fish (on which the hogs lived) that it was nauseating, and a great many could not eat it. This mode of living on salt pork, with no vegetables, brought on a strange malady. I visited one of my neighbors who was very sick, and then I discovered the nature of the complaint."

"What was it?"

"Scurvy."

"Scurvy!"

"Yes."

"Ah, that was terrible! What was done for it?"

"One man who saw the case, and who had become familiar with it in the army, recommended raw potatoes grated in vinegar. But where were the potatoes to come from? There were none in this section, and even if there had been, there was no money to buy them with. It so happened that one of the settlers, who was called to Visalia as a juror, had invested two dollars of his jury-fees in early potatoes for seed. They were from a second crop, and were about as large as walnuts. This man's sister had planted them near a well, where water could be used on them, (you know nothing would grow here then without water) intending to raise seed for the following year; but they had been planted only about two weeks, when the increase of scurvy compelled the woman to take them up. She grated them in vinegar, and gave this mixture as a medicine."

"Such things are inconceivable."

"Well, the experience of that year proved that nothing

could be done without water. But how could water be brought into this desert without money? To such straits were we driven that many of us depended on our guns for a living. We would shoot wild geese and ducks, and pick them, and take the feathers to Visalia and exchange them for provisions. Many others went away and worked through the summer months. They would bring back seed, only to see the drouth kill it. The third year there was some grain raised in one of the settlements; and when it was threshed, the farmers who had not gone away found employment as threshers, and some of us were thus enabled to obtain seed without crossing the mountains. I knew one woman who cooked for the threshers at several farms, and she received ten sacks of wheat in payment for her services; but on taking it home, she discovered that it was half barley. She and her children worked at night and picked out the wheat from the barley, grain by grain, until they had one sack of clean wheat. She planted this, and the drouth killed it. Such was the experience of all of us for five consecutive years. We tried to induce others to settle on the lands with us, thinking this would increase the chances of constructing a ditch in which water for irrigating the lands could be brought from King's River; but nobody would come."

"Why didn't you leave?"

"Because we had faith in the country, which we believed needed only irrigation. Besides, a highway to market was about to be opened, and we wanted to be the pioneers in the prosperity we believed awaited us. Further than that, we were too poor to go elsewhere. If we could have foreseen the robbery and false dealing to which we would be subjected, we should have gone in any event. After great privations, we succeeded in having a ditch surveyed, and then we commenced work; and then, when there was a prospect of water, people settled both public and so-called railroad lands, preferring the latter on account of the longer time for settlement proposed by the railroad company. The majority of those who settled on public land were compelled to borrow money with which to meet payments, and had to pay a heavy interest—from three to five per cent. a month."

"Is it possible?"

"This kept many so poor that by the time water was procured their lands had passed into the hands of others."

"How could men who were so poor afford to spend their time in digging ditches?"

"Many of us had nothing to eat but beans, coarse bread made of cracked corn, roasted barley in place of coffee, and wild honey that we found in the timber; and I have known these men to work all day in the main ditch, and build their own side-ditches by moonlight, so anxious were they to get water as soon as it could be had. Look at this vast network of canals and ditches. They bear eloquent witness to the suffering that was borne in digging them."

"You were all right after you got the water?"

"By no means. The first season the water came down there was hard work to make the ditches carry it, as they were continually breaking. Repairing these damages kept the men busy all the time, and consequently the women and children had to work in the fields from morning till night. That woman you see in the house to the left cultivated thirty acres of corn with one man's assistance. My daughter and I dug a fence-ditch around our hundred and sixty acres of land, my daughter working as hard as I. I know another girl who helped her father in a similar manner; and you must consider that these were girls who had never been accustomed to such work."

"Noble women!" exclaimed the stranger, with enthusiasm.

"Noble women, did you say? Ah, my dear sir! I can give you but a feeble idea of how noble these women of Mussel Slough are. I have mentioned only a few instances, and I could name hundreds. The sun never shone on nobler women; and in the darkest days, when men, worn and hungry, entered their cabins to eat the coarse food that was all the women had to offer them, there were the bright faces and cheering words of women to nerve the men against the despair and hunger that threatened to take the strength from their arms. You may well say, 'Noble women.'"

The stranger bowed his head reverently, and pretended not to see the tears that glistened in Newton's eyes.

"Men," continued Newton, "could not have been hired to undergo the privations and hardships that these people suffered. They were working for cheap homes. They knew that, in order to secure them, they must go a long way ahead of the market; but we never dreamed of being robbed of what we had honestly earned and suffered for."

"I don't fully understand your allusions to robbery."

"I shall explain that presently. I know there has been

a great deal of scoffing at what is termed these 'starve-to-death stories'; but we who have suffered know too well what hunger is. Well, other ditches were constructed, the desert was changed into a garden, and people flocked to the country. It would be hard for you to believe that this country has ever been a desert, and that only a handful of men, with muscle and energy and hope, brought about such a change. It is now the garden spot of California."

"It certainly is," said the stranger.

"But what encouragement have we to improve the lands further, and set out trees and vines, when we must pay for transportation, to this same company that is going to rob us of our homes, two-thirds of what we make?"

"Is it possible?"

"Why, we in Mussel Slough are not alone in that. It is the curse of the entire San Joaquin Valley. Even if this company should make a gift of this land to the people, the land still would have been earned a hundred times over by hardships and unknown sufferings, to say nothing of the vast tracts of surrounding land that these hardships and sufferings have rendered valuable to the railroad company, and that will soon be offered at enormous prices."

"And what about the robbery?"

"The railroad company issued circulars, offering the lands at vague prices. The offer was accepted, and acted upon in good faith. We could not pay for the land then, as the company could not give us titles, the patents not having been received. Subsequently it issued a circular to us, informing us that we would not be charged for the improvements we had made. And now that we have rendered the land very valuable, the company is taking steps to make us pay a greatly increased price."

"Impossible!"

"And that is not all: it knows well enough that many or all of us will refuse to pay the increased price, and so it is seeking men who will buy the land from the company, and then commence suits in ejectment. You are one of the men selected for that purpose."

The stranger's face perceptibly flushed with indignation and shame, and he hastened to say:

"You may depend upon it, gentlemen, that I will not be a party to any such outrage."

"A meeting will be held at Hanford to-day, when the settlers will organize for self-protection. We are determined not to submit to the outrage, if there is any justice in the courts. Still, the corporations have become so powerful that we can hope for little. If this company had not felt pretty sure of its hold on the courts, this high-handed outrage would not have been attempted."

The stranger was enraptured at the scene that lay around him as the three pursued their way.

Graham was thoughtful and reserved, having taken no part in the conversation. He knew that every word that Newton had spoken was the truth, and that all that could be said had not been spoken. He determined to place himself between the weak and the strong, and he did not for a moment quail before the dangerous undertaking of opposing a power that overshadowed even the law.

CHAPTER XIII.

A DUEL WITH DEATH.

THE log, pushed over the bluff by Covill, did not perform its deadly work as thoroughly as Covill had intended; but it would have been infinitely more merciful if it had killed its victim outright. Instead of that, it merely pinned him to the ground, having failed to fall directly upon his body. He was awakened from his heavy sleep by something that came down upon him and caught him in a terrible trap. He gave a short, sharp scream of agony, and then became unconscious.

The log had merely fallen across his right leg, between the knee and the foot, crushing the two bones, and holding him firmly as a vise. All his other members were free. Both of the bones of his lower right leg were broken transversely in three places—at the point directly between the log and the ground, and also at points a few inches on either side of the first fracture. In this manner the two broken sections of each bone formed two obtuse angles, the ends being driven down at the vertex through the thick muscles of the calf, and forced upward at the other extremities through the skin. This was less noticeable on that side of the log on which was his foot, which was slightly raised above the ground.

In other words, that part of his leg beneath the heavy mass was curved downward, and crushed flat upon the hard ground. In addition to the transverse fractures already mentioned, the bones were split longitudinally into innumerable splinters, the sharp ends of which protruded through the badly lacerated flesh.

The blood spurted freely.

Harris soon recovered consciousness, and he instinctively made a mad effort to push the log away, as a wounded bear will bite the spot where the bullet strikes. This attempt developed an unexpected and disheartening fact. He found that he could barely reach the log with the tips of his fingers, and that he could throw no force against it. Any one who has tried the experiment knows that it is painful even to sit upright if the knees are not bent, as the muscles on the under side of the legs are thus brought into unnatural tension. Even if Harris could have reached the log, its immense weight precluded the possibility of moving it. Thus was he inexorably held a prisoner, to die alone on the plains, in a boundless solitude of silence—a terrible death!

Having made the discovery that he could not move the log, he looked wildly around for Covill, who was nowhere to be seen. Then he called in a loud and despairing voice for his companion. There was no response but a mocking echo from the other bank of the river. Then the terrible truth burst upon his mind. He knew that Covill had intended to murder him in his sleep; and when he realized this, and reflected on the awful fate that awaited him, he rent the air with frightful curses, and invoked upon his murderer's head the deepest damnation that Heaven can send.

Next, he placed his hands firmly on the ground a little forward of his shoulders, and gave a strong, steady pull backward for liberty; for he was determined not thus to die if there was the least chance of escape; and even at that moment, maddened though he was with pain, he thought of the great work that he had marked out before him.

The torture arising from the vain effort increased his suffering. The protruding bones, forced back by the straightening, cut still longer gashes in the flesh, and divided the muscles into shreds. His sufferings were indescribable. Every one of the hundreds of lacerated nerves cried out in anguish. He fortified his will to bear the pain with all the grim determination of a strong man in a desperate extremity. He shouted aloud for help. There was no human being except Covill within twenty miles. His face was ghastly pale. Every nerve quivered and vibrated. The muscles of the arms and breast twitched and writhed. His face underwent horrible contortions, and took on strange grimaces. His fingers grappled the hard ground, tearing his nails and starting the blood. He groaned in a half-audible way, but the groan was, more than anything else, a rasping, hissing whisper, the burden of which was:

"O God! O God!"

With a powerful mastery of self that is possessed by few natures, he put forth every stupendous effort of a strong will, and brought his reasoning faculties under control.

This effort was combated by involuntary movements of his muscular system in rebellion. There was a spasmodic action in the throat, much like that produced by sobbing. There was a violent and painful throbbing in the region of the stomach. There was a sudden jerking in the muscles of the spine, extending upward, and drawing his head forcibly back. There was a contraction of the muscles of the injured leg, drawing him toward the log, bending his knee, and causing the bones to grate and grind.

His will was first directed to the quelling of these disturbances, and he partially succeeded. Then he directed his mind to a contemplation of the possibility of escaping from this terrible prison. In the mean time, it was necessary to stanch the flow of blood, which was filling his trousers leg like a bag. He had a crude knowledge of elementary surgery, and this came to his assistance.

With his pocket-knife he cut away the trousers leg, and then the blood streamed from the wound to the ground. He knew that the crimson blood, which came in spurts at intervals of less than a second, was from the ruptured arteries, and that the hemorrhage could be checked by tightly binding the leg above the wound. The odor of this warm blood produced nausea. He cut off his pantaloons, and made the left leg into a kind of rope. He passed this rope under the injured leg a short distance above the knee, brought it around, formed a slip-knot, held one end against the log with his left foot, while he pulled upon the other end with his hands, and thus compressed the leg. He watched the effect. The flow was less copious, but it was not checked. It still was dangerous. Then he firmly secured the rope around his left foot, brought the other end around his neck, and then slowly straightened himself. Thus all his strength was thrown upon the rope, which sank into the muscles, wrinkling the skin, and causing the flesh to purse up on either side. Then with his right hand he held the knot, and with the left removed the rope from his neck and foot, passed the rope around two or three times, and secured the knot. This improvised rope, being made of stout cotton cloth, was very strong.

He again looked at the bleeding. The blood, which now meagerly flowed in small, regular streams, was dark and thick, and unlike the former crimson flow. He knew the hemorrhage was not dangerous, as it came from veins below the cord, and not from arteries.

This accomplished, the gloomy fact confronted him that he was merely delaying the end, and arranging for a longer period of maddening torture—a selection between a quick death by hemorrhage, and hours upon hours of pain, fever, thirst, inflammation, gangrene, putrefaction—an appalling death! He realized this, and reflected upon it. Death held him a living prisoner. What was to be done? Meanwhile, that portion of his leg below the cord was rapidly enlarging, and was taking on a dark color.

A thought occurred to him. He might burrow under the log with his knife, and thus release his mangled leg. He found he could make a commencement, and that was all, the difficulty lying in his inability to reach far enough. Besides, every movement intensified the torture, and every pang sapped so much of his strength. The pain was devouring him alive. Suddenly he was stunned by a powerful and unexpected blow. His heart sank, and then bounded. His eyelids quivered, and his eyes rolled upward. His fingers clutched the ground more desperately. It was not an external blow, but an internal; not a blow to the body, but to the mind. It was a thought, sudden, ghastly, and revolting, that stole upon him, and stabbed him unawares.

It was the idea of self-amputation. At first he avoided it, for it weakened him, performing the relaxing and sickening office of an emetic; then he listened to it; and finally he looked it squarely in the face. He possessed remarkable nerve. He decided upon this plan as his only recourse, and as an inevitability. To accept an inevitability is to become resigned; and absolute resignation centers in but one thing—death. When resignation thus comes about, it is through a painless operation of the mind, involving an expenditure of no considerable vital force, and calling for the exercise of no grander resources than such as are found in any mediocre mental organization. To choose between death and its temporary alternative, however, requires the existence of some of the grandest traits of human nature. The suicide lacks them, because he lacks courage. Two of these traits are unconquerable will and unflinching fearlessness.

The sufferer had no anæsthetic, no drug for producing coagulation, no amputating knife, no saw, no threads with which to tie up the arteries, no appliances for stitching, no lint, no bandages. He had only his pocket-knife. It was very old. The solitary blade was dull, worn narrow, and with rounded and blunt edge. The cheeks (that part through which the rivet passed) were slightly sprung apart, causing the blade to be loose in the handle. The rivet was nearly worn through. The spring was weak, so that the weight of the blade was almost sufficient to cause the knife to close. Nevertheless, he believed the knife would be serviceable enough to cut the leg at the upper end of the fracture, where the bone was already broken.

Having accepted the situation, he proceeded. A grave difficulty then presented itself. While he could, with his left hand on the ground, support himself in a half-recumbent position, there was, without this support, a painful strain on the muscles of the neck, chest, abdomen, and legs; and he required the assistance of his left hand in the operation. Furthermore, the unsteady, jerky motion of his body in this strain increased the pain to an unbearable degree. And still further, he found it impossible to reach, for a sufficient length of time, that part of his leg on which he intended to perform the operation. This was a serious and disheartening obstacle; for without a saw he could not hope to cut through the sound bone within easy reach.

He studied the problem, and solved it. He reflected that a surgeon never amputates at a joint if he can possibly avoid it, for obvious reasons: there is no muscular tissue to which the "flap" may adhere; the circulation of the blood is meager; the absorbents act slowly and insufficiently; suppuration may become gangrene; there is no fleshy cushion to protect the overlapping skin from contact with the unyielding bone; there is greater exposure of the end of the bone to variations of heat and cold; there is great difficulty in stopping the mouths of the arteries; the severed tendons are drawn up by the contraction of the muscles, leaving a still greater exposure of bone, straining the skin drawn over the end, and tending to tear open the healing wound.

Harris knew these things in an imperfect way. He parleyed with death, and dallied with eternity—gaining time, and yet consuming it; for time, though it led to death, was none the less thought, and thought might be life. Having calculated his own resources and those of the enemy, he saw his way to possible victory, and opened an aggressive fight. But the patience of death is its strongest tactics. It must be combated with boldness as well as cunning; taken unawares, flanked, harassed, attacked in the rear, charged in front. The skillful physician is daring as well as cautious.

Bracing every nerve against the dread assault, Harris made a bold, strong stroke with the edge of the knife across the leg, about three inches below the knee-joint. The skin squirmed, and then slipped from under the blade uninjured. The knife was too dull. He whetted it on the sole of his left shoe as best he could, thus making the edge at the point rather sharp. He felt the edge with his thumb, and was satisfied. Then he caught the handle firmly, prevented the possible closing of the knife on his fingers by including a portion of the blade in his grasp, compressed his lips, half closed his eyes, and with the point of the blade made a quick, glancing stroke downward on the right side of his leg below the knee. The skin parted smoothly. He ground his teeth with the pain.

After resting a moment, and calling out an extra reserve of fortitude, he inserted the blade at the lower end of the incision, took a firm hold, steadied the knife, gave it the proper direction, and ripped the skin around his leg as far as he could reach.

His face became more pinched, his nostrils expanded, and his upper lip twitched convulsively. After resting a moment, he inserted the blade in the upper end of the incision, pushed it under the skin a short distance in order to give it a better start, and proceeded to cut around toward the left. In this position he found the cutting awkward, and his arm had less leverage. The knife was dull, considerable force being necessary to propel it. It tore as much as it cut.

During all this time he had borne the weight of his body on his left arm, employing the right in cutting. Not a groan escaped him; but his breathing was short and quick and spasmodic. It was merely strangled groans.

When with his right hand he had cut with accuracy as far as he could reach, he lay down, shifted the knife to his left hand, raised himself upon his right arm, and with his left hand completed the incision around the leg.

Then he lay down again, and rested; having done which, he again raised himself on his right arm, and with the knife in his left hand cut the skin in a straight line on the inner side of the leg from the first incision to the knee-joint, having first ascertained by careful examination the exact locality of the joint. With his right hand he made a similar incision on the opposite side, in this way shaping the "flap" of skin that was to cover the end of the bone.

The next step was to separate from the flesh that portion of the skin between the joint and the circumscribing incision. He commenced at the outer corner of the upper flap, by slipping the blade between the skin and the flesh; but the pain therefrom was excruciating, and the process was slow. He arrested his hand, and reflected. The knife was slippery with blood.

A ghastly idea occurred to him, and he proceeded to put it into execution. At the same moment he hit on a timely invention.

He required both hands in doing the thing he contemplated; and so he made his rope longer, being compelled to use one shirt sleeve for the purpose, tied the ends of the rope together, put his head through one end of the loop and his left foot through the other, and by pushing his foot against the tree, the rope was made to raise him by the neck to nearly a sitting posture. In this way the lacerated muscles were relieved of strain; and both hands being free, he could work with greater ease and rapidity.

With his knife he performed the painful operation of loosening the skin above the incision for a distance of nearly an inch all around. Having completed this, he laid the knife aside.

He then with both hands firmly grasped the loose edge of the upper flap, and allowed the rope to slip from the toes of his left foot, being thus enabled to throw the weight of his body upon his arms.

He drew a deep inspiration, ground his teeth, gave his head a sullen shake, like an angered bull in a fight, and with a pull that was quick, sure, and strong, he tore up the skin from the circumscribing incision to the knee. In this horrible operation a hundred nerves were torn asunder, and each cried out in dire agony.

The suffering exhausted him, and for a time he lay prone on the ground.

Then he returned to the bloody assault, in a similar manner tearing up the under flap. The two flaps were thus folded back upon his leg above the knee. To protect the lower flap from the dirt, he cut off the remaining sleeve, and spread it on the ground underneath his knee.

The most painful part of the operation was over, but the most difficult remained to be done. The sufferer found himself sick, and growing weak every moment. An intense thirst consumed him. He must hasten.

He readjusted the rope around his left foot, and again held himself in a sitting posture. The difficulty that then presented itself was indeed serious, and perhaps insurmountable. If he had been so situated that he could bend the knee freely, and thus effect advantageous openings for the insertion of the knife, the amputation would not have been so difficult. Selecting the spot just below the patella, or knee-cap, in order thus to secure a greater length to the tendon, as an allowance for muscular contraction, he proceeded to cut. The knife struck the large, strong tendon, and glanced aside. He could not cut it. Again did he whet the knife on his shoe, and again did he attack the tendon. By pressing down the blade with all the strength he could command, and drawing it back and forth like a saw, he caused the thick tendon gradually to part. It was a painful operation; for, although the tendon was not traversed nor accompanied by appreciable nerves, the jarring and straining caused by the pressure of the knife caused great pain to the injured parts.

On the parting of the tendon, he experienced a strange sensation. His knee endeavored to bend of its own accord. This was caused by the tension on the tendons underneath, there no longer being a counteracting force above. Harris saw that he had committed a blunder by not severing the latter first, as the bending of the knee wrenched the mangled part. He hastily repaired this damage by cutting the lower tendons, severing them about an inch below the joint. This relieved him greatly.

He then commenced to cut the intricate network of ligaments that formed a powerful guard around the joint. In this mass were concentrated a large number of the nerves that ran to the foot, after the manner of wires in the main wire-box of a bell annunciator. Any violation to them was consequently a concentration of nearly all the pain that the foot could suffer. He severed them all, though with suppressed groans and gasps.

It was a tedious process, but he was becoming expert with the knife. As he had expected, the tendons drew up as he cut them, and the gap widened as he deepened it.

With little trouble he removed the patella, and laid it aside. Underneath it he found a bed of ligaments, and he penetrated these to the bone.

The joint was then visible. The articulation (as a joint is called) of the knee is what is termed a hinge, to distinguish it from ball-and-socket joints. The ends of the bones coming together to form the joint are packed with tough cartilage. Harris ran the point of his knife along the crevice in the hinge, below and above; but the bones were still inseparable.

He tried to force the straight blade into the tough cartilage intervening; but, as this cartilage rounded with the curve of the joint, the blade was forced to bend.

Suddenly a great calamity befell him. The rivet snapped, and the handle and blade fell apart.

He dropped the useless handle in dismay. His heart sank. His sword broken, the enemy could now run him through. He was now defenseless, and death was hard pressing him.

After this momentary depression came a strange reaction. A terrible, desperate fury sprung up in his breast. His face had a wild, haggard, demoniacal look. A kind of mad delirium seized him—dark, unfathomable, and furious. He was brought to bay. Instead of any longer having an intelligent plan, he gave up to the most desperate exasperation. He began to concentrate his remaining strength in one grand onslaught, that would crush and tear and lacerate, and scatter to the winds, regardless of everything, fearful of nothing. He lurched violently and frantically, and tugged madly at the mangled limb. Still the joint refused to yield.

But he made a strange discovery. It no longer pained him to disturb the fracture. To make sure of this, he turned about and mangled it worse. It did not increase the dull and constant pain. At first it alarmed him, for he thought he was past sensibility; but he soon dispelled this fear by experiments on other parts of his body.

It gave him a new idea and calmed him. He put this idea into operation. He arose, and stood as nearly upright as possible, his bended left leg sustaining his weight.

There was a terrible determination in his face. Concentrating all his strength in one supreme effort, he straightened himself, and violently wrenched the joint asunder.

Three hours later a sheep-herder found him sitting on the bank of the river, nearly naked, and covered from head to foot with blood. His eyes rolled wildly, and he grinned and gibbered and chattered—hopelessly insane.

CHAPTER XIV.

A RUPTURE.

THE years dragged slowly by, and the spring of 1880 was at hand. Graham had not accepted the proffered situation; for, after mature consideration, he had decided that it would be better for him to continue in the old life.

Meanwhile, what had become of poor Nellie, whose pretty head was turned a few years ago by the dazzling view of life that the money and influence of her rich friends had opened to her gaze and enjoyment? She was not yet married to John, for John had not recovered the treasure, and was a poor man still. Indeed, there were other sufficient reasons why she had not married John. The old sympathy that had existed between them was gone. Nellie was no longer the Nellie that John had known. She no longer talked over his plans with him, nor gave him bright words of encouragement through the trials that had beset him, and that still rendered his future dark. On the contrary, she added to his sorrows with her upbraidings and complaints. The poison had entered her life. Dark shadows had crept in, and driven out the sunshine and the bright hopefulness.

She was discontented with her humble lot, and longed to be in reality one of those who go to make up that society of California whose standing is on a basis of money. No rupture had taken place between her and John, but it was sure to come. A gulf had been created between them. John, with his patient, charitable disposition, had often tried to convince her of the hollowness of the life she longed for; but even at that late day he had never suspected the true motives that led to Nellie's temporary adoption by her new friends. She had never ceased reproaching him for refusing the situation that had been offered him, and that she had urged him to accept with all her winning eloquence. But he would not, and that was the end of it.

Nor was that all. He had warmly espoused the cause of the Mussel Slough settlers, which had taken a more serious turn during the past few years. Nellie's sympathies were not with them.

"Why, John," she once said petulantly, "those people are not worth getting into trouble for. You ought to hear Judge Harriott and those great men who sometimes go to his house talk about those poor fools in Mussel Slough. They make all manner of fun of them. Judge Harriott— you know he is a manager or something—said that it is really amusing to see those ignorant creatures in Mussel Slough trying to fight the railroad company, which can tie them all in a bundle, and throw them into the fire. What do you trouble yourself about them for, John?"

"Nellie," John replied earnestly, "those people in Mussel Slough have been shamefully wronged, and I am in a position similar to theirs. Do you suppose we will be such cowards as to sit down and see our homes taken from us, even if the power that is attempting the outrage is rich enough to buy the courts, the legislature, and the congressional committees that assisted to rob the people of these lands? Why, Nellie, it would be difficult for a disinterested spectator to believe that such things are done in a country where every man is supposed to be free. If we quietly submit to these wrongs, what, in the name of God, is to become of us?"

"But, John, you don't understand. The men you speak of in that harsh way are good, charitable, honest men; and they have done so much for the country!"

"Because it paid them to do it, Nellie."

"It is not right to talk in that way, John."

"Nellie, Nellie! have they so far poisoned your mind that you are blind to the truth? You think they are good men; yet how could good men make promises and offer inducements to poor people, and then, when these poor people have rendered a piece of property immensely valuable, they are called upon to give it up, or pay in money what they have paid already a hundred times over in sufferings that you can't imagine?"

"They have been very kind to me, John; and surely they don't expect me to be of any service to them?"

"How do you know, Nellie? Don't you know that placing people under obligations is one of the regular departments of their business, as well as employing lobbyists, lawyers, and political managers who corrupt conventions and buy the votes of needy and unscrupulous men? Don't you know why I refused to accept the situation they offered me?"

"No: I know only that it would have been a great thing for you, and that some day you would be a rich man."

John paced the floor in considerable agitation, and thus expostulated:

"Nellie, there was a motive in that offer. Do you imagine for a moment that they care anything for me, or would give me a crust of bread if I were starving? No, Nellie! They naturally reasoned that the situation would, if I accepted it, have put a gag in my mouth. Why, Nellie, see how successfully they have practiced that very ruse right here in our section! There are a great many men here who sympathize with the railroad company and curse the poor settlers. How did it come about? Through some favor that the railroad company granted. I admit, Nellie, that it is a very difficult matter for a man to withstand many of the temptations that are offered; but, Nellie, what is money when manhood is gone? Here we are, a mere handful of men, opposed to the strongest power in the country—the power of money; the power that lies behind the law and courts; the power whose sole object is the accumulation of greater wealth and greater power; a power that is determined, with the aid of the machinery of the law, to crush out all semblance of opposition, and that directs its most powerful shafts against those who are least able to withstand them.

"I say we are a mere handful of men, because the time

has not yet come when wrongs have become so great and so general that a larger and more united band of the oppressed feel the crushing weight of the heel that grinds them; but that we are few is no reason that we should be cowards. We have God and right on our side, Nellie. We have on our side the prayers of the widow and the cries of the children for bread. We have on our side right against might, justice against infamous wrongs, honesty against theft, industry against robbery, hunger against a feast; and before God, Nellie, we will fight for our rights to the bitter end; and other people, seeing our brave little band standing up and defiantly opposing a power that is great enough to buy a nation, will flock to our standard, and maintain their rights as secured by the Constitution of the United States—the right of all men to acquire property and enjoy life. If no stand is ever made against these outrages practiced by the rich on the poor, what will become of this country? Even now, Nellie, money is the great power in this country; and with a single stroke of the pen, a few rich men can stop every railroad and factory in the country, and send millions of people out upon the highways clamoring for bread."

"Then why don't they do it?"

"Because they dare not. Because hungry, red-handed violence would take them by the throat, and make them disgorge the fortunes they have made out of the miseries of poor men! Because the sun would rise some morning and discover them dangling between heaven and earth, with a rope around their necks!"

John was pale with excitement, and Nellie quaked under

the ferocity that appeared in his face. Nevertheless, she said:

"John, Judge Harriott says that the corporations are very lenient that they don't send to the penitentiary men who talk like that."

John was calmer in a moment.

"I know it, Nellie. I know they laugh at us in our weakness, and have great fun at our writhings under the misfortunes that are thrust upon us. But the day is coming, Nellie, when these wrongs will be righted. I hope it will not be through blood, though I fear that blood will be spilled. I fear that it must be spilled before the people are sufficiently aroused to the danger that assails them—the danger of cold, cruel, grasping money. There is good ground for hope that the people will soon be awakened. We are not all who suffer. There are the thousands of corporation laborers who are compelled to renounce their manhood; there are those who have angered the corporations, and who are hounded out of the country; there are those who must pay as a tribute to the corporations all they can earn by hard labor; there are the merchants who are bound under contracts to ship all their goods by rail, to the end that ocean transportation may be driven from the seacoast of California; there are the outspoken newspapers from which the corporations compel merchants to withhold advertising patronage; there are the great masses of voters who are cheated and cajoled into voting for men whom their respective parties nominate in the interest of the corporations. Why, Nellie, there is hardly a man, woman, or child in all this country who does not feel, directly or indirectly, the weight of this curse. A reaction is bound to come. People must, in simple self-protection, organize to defeat this monster."

"It seems to me, John," said Nellie, somewhat overawed, "that if the corporations are driving people to such an extremity, the rich men would, for the sake of their own interests, change their policy."

"Nellie, that which makes a man a robber will cause him to continue a thief. These rich men are following the dictates of their natures. Furthermore, they are so inflated with power that they no longer deem it necessary to be conciliatory and just. What have they to fear? Surely not the government, which their money can control; and surely not the people, for the people are not organized; and besides, they are cowardly. But mark my words, Nellie, the time is coming when the people will rise up in their majesty, and crush this power that is stronger than the law. It may be through blood, but I hope not. Still, history shows that such wrongs are righted only through blood, or through some local catastrophe that may be sufficient to arouse the whole people."

Nellie sat stubborn and offended. She could not believe that John was right, but attributed his remarks to the influence of the men with whom he had associated so much recently. She knew not, poor, simple Nellie, that she was among those who had been marked for the slaughter.

"Nellie," continued John, "I would not be a servant for the railroad company for all the money it would pay me.

Don't you remember that shameful case the other day, when poor Simpson's young widow sued the railroad company for damages? Her husband was a brakeman, and he was killed by reason of a defect in the brake-wheel. Well, the railroad company had a great crowd of railroad men as witnesses, who all swore that Simpson came to his death through his own carelessness, although the brake-wheel itself showed that it was fatally defective. Those witnesses perjured themselves—as they always do in such cases—to retain their positions. One man, who had the courage and honor to tell the truth, was soon afterwards discharged; and you know that as a result of his testimony he couldn't find employment on any railroad in this country, and was finally compelled to cross the Rocky Mountains. In spite of all that testimony, the jury brought in a verdict for the widow; and it is such things as these that give us hope in the people. Did you ever reflect upon what that verdict meant? It meant this: We know that these witnesses swore untruths, and the law of every country declares that we shall make due allowance for the testimony of the servants of corporations, for the reason that corporations have great power, and can injure a servant who testifies against them. We do not blame these witnesses, but we pity them from the bottom of our hearts. We pity rather than blame any condition to which humanity can be brought, in which manhood and honor are sold for the bread that keeps the wolf from the door; but we do blame—and this verdict bears us testimony—the power that is so abused in that it enslaves the soul of a man, and blackmails his conscience with threats of hunger."

"But, John, I have heard these gentlemen say that many things are done wrong in their name without their knowledge or consent. How can you blame them for that?"

"When a knowledge of these wrongs comes to them, do they discharge the servants who committed them? By no means! These are notorious facts, Nellie. We do not blame the servants so much, because the system that controls them compels them to do wrong; and having become once ensnared, they cannot shake off the yoke."

John and Nellie frequently had such conversations; but only harm came out of them. The breach between John and Nellie was steadily widening, for a little kindness and much frippery had won Nellie's heart from the people.

Matters were in this condition when Nellie was again invited to San Francisco. She told John. For the first time he gently but firmly opposed her; and Nellie, high-spirited and brave, resented the interference, and a rupture ensued.

"Nellie," said John, pale and earnest, "since you wish and declare that all is over between us, so be it; but I hope and believe that your heart is not changed, and that you will come back to me. You choose between me and these people who are seeking to crush me. Very well. You are no longer my friend."

Flushed and angry, Nellie left him. As she was leaving, John added:

"This is another wrong, Nellie—and the greatest of all—that I will lay up against my enemies—your friends."

CHAPTER XV.

AN APPARITION.

IT had been a long time since Graham heard from Covill. The new dangers that assailed Graham eclipsed his individual and private interests, the welfare of others being concerned. The complications that had arisen in land matters were of greater urgency than was Graham's quest for the stolen treasure. In the latter matter he had not progressed a step. Although he knew who committed the murder, he was still in ignorance of the whereabouts of the murderers; and as yet had no inkling of the priest or the location of the Lone Tree fortune. But this did not cause him great distress. He was young, and could bide his time. The whole man, however, had undergone a change. He had now become sullen and almost despondent. The loss of Nellie, which he believed was irrevocable and irretrievable, had taken the heart and spirit out of him, and left him morose and rebellious. It is a man in such a condition who is prepared for any desperate deed that may present itself.

Besides, a terrible uneasiness had taken possession of him on Nellie's account. She had been gone a month, and yet none of her friends had heard from her. Her uncle had written to her several times, and still no answer came. He had appealed to her friends, and they had paid no attention to his letters.

At last came Monday, the 10th of May, and still there was no news from Nellie; but in looking over the list of letters advertised in a San Francisco newspaper, Graham saw that uncalled-for letters awaited Nellie. This was an extraordinary circumstance, and he immediately went to Nellie's uncle with the information. Mr. Foster was no less surprised than Graham. Naturally he was anything but suspicious; but the fact that Nellie's letters were advertised, coupled with the other fact of her long and unusual silence, alarmed the old man so greatly that he decided to visit San Francisco at once and look for his niece.

He and Graham were walking slowly toward Graham's house, when they met an apparition on the road. It was an old, old man, with long white hair and beard, and dressed in ragged and dirty clothes. He looked ill and emaciated. So pitable was his plight as he sat by the roadside, and such a wild and hungry look he had through the dusty, shaggy white hair that fell over his shoulders, that the two men instinctively halted.

"Good morning, sir," said Graham, kindly.

The wretched old man flared up in a moment; and grasping a primitive crutch that lay at his side, he raised it aloft with a threatening and defiant air, and shouted:

"Stand back, there!"

He looked like a wild animal brought to bay.

"Stand back," he shouted, with a terrible oath. "I'm an old man, and have but one leg; but I'm a match for you both, if you don't sneak on me while I'm asleep. Stand back, I tell you, or, by God, I'll make you!"

The two men gazed at him in astonishment, and then Graham whispered:

"He's insane."

"It's a lie!" shouted the old man, as he scrambled to an upright position on his one leg. "They all say that, but I tell you it's a lie. They poke their heads at one another, and whisper, 'He's crazy'; but I tell you, it's a lie. I was buried twenty years ago, and have just got up out of the grave. Because an old man is starving to death, and gets so weak he can't hobble along the road, they say he's crazy. I'm *not* crazy; and, what's more, you can't take me alive. Ah, you've hunted for me for twenty years, have you? Well, what of it? I was dead for eighteen years. You've found me, haven't you? Then take me, if you dare. Take me! Ha, ha, ha! Take me, I say. You can't do it, because you are brave men. I'm afraid of cowards, but I'm not afraid of brave men. A coward murders you while you sleep. Ha, ha! But I ain't asleep now, d——n you, nor dead either; I'm wide awake. Do you hear that? Wide awake and alive, I say; both eyes open, and a good stout crutch in my hands. Stand back, there, or I'll knock your brains out"; and with that, he dashed at them with uplifted crutch; but, being ill-used to his infirmity, he fell flat in the dirt.

Graham picked him up and sat him upright, and soothingly said:

"There, now, be quiet. We are friends, and wouldn't hurt you for all the world. You wouldn't strike your friends, you know."

"Friends!" shrieked the old man—"friends! You are not my friends. I haven't any friends. I never had but one friend, and he tried to murder me in my sleep. Ah, if I could find him, wouldn't I cut out his heart! Ah! ah! wouldn't I drink his blood, and gouge out his eyes by the roots, and strew his entrails on the ground! Friends! You are no friends of mine!"

"Yes, we are. Now, be calm, and let me tell you something. There are some men down the road, and they are looking for you."

"What!" screamed the old man, in an agony of terror. "Where are they?"

"They will soon be along; and unless you come with us they will catch you and put you in jail."

"In jail!" shouted the old man, whiter than ever with fear. "Don't let them take me," he begged piteously; and then he seized Graham's hand, and while the tears streamed down his face, he begged:

"Oh, don't let them take me! They've been hunting me for twenty years, and haven't caught me yet, because I was dead so long! And they have a ghost to help them—a ghost that knows me, that has known me for twenty long years—long years, don't you hear? In the name of God, don't let them take me! But they wouldn't harm a poor old man like me, would they?"

"I think they would," urged Graham. "You had better come to my house now, before they find you."

The old man lost no time in getting meekly upon his foot and crutch, and following Graham. He muttered to himself, and frequently cast a fearful look behind him, and shook his head continually.

When they arrived at Graham's house, John bade him enter. The demented old man—for he was more demented than insane—peered cautiously into the room before he entered it, and then he hobbled through the door-way, and dropped wearily into a chair that Graham placed for him.

Graham's grandmother was attending to some duties in the yard, and John brought the poor old cripple something to eat, and placed it on a table before him. The old man looked hungrily at the tempting dinner, and was about to commence devouring it, when he started back in dismay

"You are going to poison me!" he said piteously.

In order to assure him that there was no such intention, Graham ate some of the food, and convinced the old man that it had not been poisoned. Somewhat reassured, the stranger, mumbling incoherently meanwhile, attacked the food mincingly; and then, forgetting his fear, he ate ravenously—ate like a dog that had been starved for a week; ate as only a human being driven almost to death by hunger can eat when food is offered; ate voraciously, cramming his mouth with food faster than he could swallow it, tearing the meat to pieces with his bony fingers, and almost choking himself. Graham talked kindly to him, and brought him this and that to eat and drink, and urged him to be patient, as he was with friends. As his hunger was gradually appeased, the old man became more moderate, and finally he ceased, having gorged to his utmost capacity. Then he looked vacantly around, and suddenly an insupportable drowsiness overcame him, and he fell asleep on the table. Fearing to disturb him, and knowing that sleep would calm his disordered mind, Graham allowed him to slumber.

The old grandmother entered the room, and Graham explained to her the presence of the stranger. They were engaged for an hour or more in a half-whispered conversation, when suddenly they were startled by a hoarse scream from the old man. They looked at him, and found him staring wildly and terror-stricken at Mrs. Graham, as if she were the Avenging Angel that had been hunting him through all the dreary years; that had followed him during the eighteen years that he passed in the other world; and that had taken human shape and followed him back to life, to hound him still.

CHAPTER XVI.

RETURNED TO LIFE.

THE fear depicted in the old man's face was terrible. He sat, aghast and speechless, gazing at Graham's grandmother; and then, without for a moment taking his gaze from the old lady's face, he felt about for his crutch, but failed to find it. Then, with his foot he felt around upon the floor, and still failed to find his crutch. Abandoning this attempt, he slowly and noiselessly arose, by placing one hand on the table and the other on the back of the chair, and attempted to gain the door without making any noise. Divining his intention, Graham stepped forward, touched him gently on the arm, and kindly said:

"Be seated, and rest yourself; we are all your friends. That lady is my grandmother, and she is glad to see you, and wouldn't harm a hair of your head."

"Wouldn't she?" whispered the old man, still gazing with terror at Mrs. Graham.

"No; she likes you, and she'll help us to keep away those men who are hunting you."

The old man started slightly as this new terror was brought to his memory, and then he whispered:

"Is she dead?'

"No; she's alive, thank God, and she wants you to sit down and rest. Don't you, grandmother?"

"Yes, John; of course I do. I wouldn't let any one harm the gentleman for anything in the world."

Her kind, sweet, soothing voice had a strange effect on the poor old cripple, in whose eyes tears commenced to gather. Then he drew John close to him, and again whispered:

"Has she forgiven me?"

"He wants to know if you have forgiven him, grandmother. You have, haven't you?"

The old lady knew of nothing that she might forgive him, but in the same sweet voice, she answered:

"O yes, John—long ago. I had even forgotten all about it. I am nothing now but a friend."

These tender words, in the good old lady's sweet, soft voice, affected the stranger so deeply that he crouched down upon the chair, and buried his face in his hands, which rested on his knees; and then he sobbed like a child.

"God knows," he stammered between his sobs, "that I shouldn't have done it for all the world if I hadn't been led into it. But I don't take any blame off my own shoulders for that. I helped him do it, and that was enough; and to-day he is a great, rich man, while I'm a poor beggar, with some people trying to murder me in my sleep, and others hunting me and driving me from pillar to post. And God knows that if I had my life to live over again I would put a knife into my own heart before I would harm a single hair of my old neighbor's head. O dear, good madam, if you'll forgive me, I'll be your slave the balance of my old life; and I'll make them give up the money that they took from him, and you shall have it for his boy. Where is his boy?" asked the old man, looking wildly around.

A light was slowly dawning upon Graham, and he asked: "Where is that money?"

"Eh!" shouted the old man, in a terrible fury. "You want it, do you? It would curse you if you had it"; and he glared angrily at Graham.

Slowly and surely the light was breaking upon Graham. Carefully he put this and that together, and the result startled him.

"What is your name?" he asked.

"My name, sir?" screamed the old man, boiling with rage. "My name is Harris. Look out, sir! If you speak that other name I'll kill you!"

Graham walked over to the old man; and taking a position directly in front of him, and eyeing him steadily, he said:

"Twenty years ago two men lived in this part of the country. They were brothers, and their name was Webster."

"It's a lie!" shouted the old man, in a desperate fury; but Graham's calm, commanding look overawed him, and made him subside.

"These brothers," continued Graham, "were killed in the mountains by Indians, about twenty years ago."

"Yes, yes! they were killed! Ha, ha, ha! and they were buried—buried deep!" laughed the old man eagerly, and rubbing his hands together. "Yes, yes! they were killed by the Indians, I say! Ha, ha, ha! killed by the Indians! Had their throats cut! Ha, ha, ha! and buried!"

"They were buried on King's River," continued Graham, calmly.

"Yes, yes, yes! Buried on King's River! Ha, ha, ha! Buried on the bank of King's River! Buried deep, deep, deep!"

"They were *not* buried on King's River," said Graham, sternly.

"Eh!"

"They were *not* buried on King's River. The coffins were filled with wood and stones, and the wood and the stones were buried on King's River."

The old cripple sat pale and speechless with terror.

"And that is not all," continued Graham, in a loud voice and with a threatening manner. "These two brothers killed a man, and robbed him, and buried the money under Lone Tree."

The old man was helpless and unresisting.

"And that is not all yet," said Graham. "Those two murderers are alive to-day, and you are one of them!"

The poor cripple, forgetting that he had himself betrayed the secret, and who had been sitting motionless, and with a look of intense anxiety and fear in his face, sank under this terrible and crushing accusation, and trembled like a beef that has received the blow of the butcher's knife.

Meanwhile, the old lady had been looking from her

grandson to the stranger with a look of indescribable wonder. Her palsied hands trembled more violently than usual, with intense excitement, as the strange revelation dawned upon her. Then a look of great horror came into her eyes as she regarded the decrepit stranger with intense loathing. She rose to her feet and tottered to John; and taking him by the arm, said:

"Don't kill him, John. God has already punished him with an affliction more awful than death."

It was well that she did this, for all the pent-up fury that had been slumbering and accumulating in John's breast for two years was nigh bursting forth in a bloody vengeance. He had guessed but half the truth. The full sequel to his midnight visit to the graveyard had not presented itself to his slow-working mind. His grandmother's words soothed him, and with an effort he calmed himself. And then he was ashamed that any thought of taking revenge upon this helpless old man had entered his mind.

With these reflections came others. This man might, after all, be the one who wrote the anonymous letter two years ago, and a visit or a word from whom John had been patiently expecting for so long.

But he had gone too far. The old man, rendered twenty years older by the tragedy through which he passed on the bank of the San Joaquin, was so completely crushed by the accusation with which John overwhelmed him that he could only sit and mumble unintelligible words. The last spark of reason was gone, and nothing but a helpless animal remained. He took the old man's hand, and talked kindly to him, endeavoring by all means in his power to recall to light the shattered senses of the cripple; but the old man looked at him with vacant eyes, and cried piteously as a child, the tears streaming down his haggard, wrinkled face, and mingling with the dust that grimed his whiskers. Bitterly did John accuse himself of his own rashness, and vainly did he strive to recover the only hope that had come in his way.

CHAPTER XVII.

THE WARNING.

NOR did Graham's efforts to bring the old man back to consciousness cease with kindly and reassuring words. Graham's anxiety increased in proportion to the extension of time in which he was unsuccessful. The old man was very feeble. His life hung by a thread, which perhaps Graham had already so strained that it might snap at any moment, and carry with its destruction every hope of discovering all the mysterious circumstances attending the murder and the secretion of the treasure. The day was wearing away, and still the old man sat in helpless imbecility. The change in Graham's feelings toward him, that ensued after this collapse of all semblance of intelligence, was perfectly natural to one of Graham's disposition, and consisted in profound pity for the old man, and a desire to do anything for him that could be done to ameliorate the distress of his condition; and this desire was apart from and in addition to his wish to utilize any knowledge of which the old man might be in possession. The conclusion forced itself upon Graham's mind, that it was his own precipitate conduct that had brought on the present condition of affairs; that beyond a doubt the old man had been led to that very spot by an intelligence which some great calamity of the mind had reduced to an instinct; that if the helpless old cripple had been treated with greater kindness, and had not been anticipated, but had been led gradually on to a full statement and confession, he would have told all that he knew, and would thus have put Graham in possession of the facts for which he had been vainly hunting for years.

Was there any way under heaven by which the lost ground could be retrieved? Was it possible that time, which softens the hardships that every blow inflicts, could come to a partial rescue of the old man's mind?

Old Webster—for such was his true name—stared blankly from one to another of the three persons who sat watching him in silence; and when Mr. Foster left, the imbecile looked longingly after him, as if a friend were deserting him in an extremity. Soon, however, he forgot that circumstance, and confined his absorbed attention to Graham and Graham's grandmother. He would glance quickly at the one who addressed him, but his face showed an utter absence of understanding. He spoke not a word, and betrayed no desire to take his departure; but it was easy to see that he was chained to his seat by fear, and that he regarded himself as a prisoner.

Insanity is of various kinds, and as regards causes is always difficult of diagnosis, though it is customary to reason backward from symptoms. In general terms, it may be said to consist in a morbid nervous excitation. It not infrequently happens that this excitation consumes the mind to such an extent that imbecility follows insanity; and such seemed to be the condition of Webster. Graham had a partial knowledge of these matters, and had always felt keen interest in reading books relating to pathological phenomena. With the information that he possessed, he determined to make an experiment.

Whisky produces a kind of temporary insanity; and in any event, it seldom fails in effecting mental or nervous excitement. Graham had read of curious experiments that had been tried upon imbecile persons with whisky; and among them he had noticed cases in which there was a temporary restoration of the mental faculties, where the destruction of the mind had not gone to the extent of a serious disarrangement of the cellular construction of the brain. He would try this experiment on the imbecile who sat staring and grinning at him.

He poured into a glass a quantity of whisky that his grandmother kept for medicinal purposes, and handing it to the old man, peremptorily ordered him to drink it. Webster took the glass with the most abject meekness, held it in his trembling hand, and while the look of fear in his face became more intense, he muttered one word:

"Poison."

"No, it is not poison. It is medicine. Drink it."

Graham's tone was not without a shade of kindness, although it was stern and emphatic. Webster drank the liquor without a moment's hesitation, placed the glass on the table, and again fixed his vacant eyes on Graham with a look of profound resignation and martyrdom. Graham anxiously watched the effect of the liquor.

He was soon rewarded. The old man's face flushed and his eyes became brighter. He sighed, turned uneasily about in his chair, and his look became wilder but less vacant.

Presently he took the glass from the table and held it toward Graham, saying:

"More."

Graham poured out a small quantity, and the old man eagerly drank it. In a few minutes more Graham's heart bounded joyfully to discover that old Webster's tongue was loosened at last.

"He tried to murder me!" said the partially intoxicated imbecile, with great excitement. "He climbed upon the bank, and threw a log down upon me while I slept."

"Who did?" asked Graham, as the old man suddenly checked himself and looked cautiously around. But he withdrew into himself, and Graham saw that some other plan than asking direct questions must be resorted to. He must encourage a statement rather than lead it.

"If I find him I will kill him," said Graham.

"Will you?" cried Webster, eagerly. "Ah, I'll help you! I'll help you cut out his heart."

"Where is he?"

"Sh—h," whispered the old man mysteriously, again looking cautiously around. Then he leaned far forward and whispered, "They are coming to-morrow."

"Are they?"

"Yes. I saw 'em last night. I watched 'em, ha ha! They didn't think a crazy old man could hear anything. Ah, ha, ha! They are going to turn 'em all out of house and home. Hey! They are going to turn 'em out, do you hear that? Turn 'em out like cattle."

"You heard them say that?" asked Graham, feeling his way, and not divining the meaning of these rambling words.

"Yes, yes, yes! Heard 'em say it. I was lying on some straw behind the house, and I heard 'em talking. O, I wasn't asleep. I never sleep."

Still Graham was unable to fathom the meaning of the old man's words.

"What are they going to turn them out for?" he asked.

"Eh?"

"What are they going to turn them out for?"

"Why, to put others in. Ha, ha, ha! To put others in."

"To put others in?"

"Yes."

"What for?"

"Eh?"

"Why do they want to put others in?"

The question puzzled the old man so much that he could merely shake his head.

"To put others in," he repeated.

Leaving this subject for future thought, and realizing the fact that the old man would soon relapse into imbecility, Graham, desiring to learn as much as possible while old Webster was in a condition to talk, asked, as he pointed to his grandmother:

"Are you afraid of this woman?"

Webster had become excited to such a degree in relating the conversation between the strangers, that he had for the moment forgotten the old lady. When his attention was again called to her by Graham, his intense fear returned, and he trembled in every limb.

"Are you afraid of her?" persisted Graham. "You need not be, for she is your friend."

"I am your friend," gently said the old lady.

This kindness touched the old man's heart at once, and he sobbed pitifully.

"You wouldn't lay it up against a poor old man, would you, ma'am?" he pleaded, between his sobs. "I wouldn't 'a' done it for all the world. And then I had to die, and they buried me deep, deep. Why, ma'am, I was buried eighteen years! I wish they hadn't brought me back. But it seems to me," he added, as though he were trying to remember something that endeavored to elude him—"it seems to me that even while I was dead I had a very hard time—a very, very hard time."

"Where is your brother?" asked Graham, bluntly.

"Dead."

"When did he die?"

"Killed by the Indians."

"And he was buried at the time you were?"

"Yes."

"Well," said Graham, "he, too, has come to life."

"Eh? What is that?" eagerly asked Webster.

"Your brother has come to life."

"To life?"

"Yes."

"My brother?"

"Yes."

The old man shook his head in gloomy doubt.

"He is a priest," said Graham.

This remark seemed unintelligible to old Webster, much to Graham's disappointment. But the thoughts of the old man were evidently very busy, for his brows were knitted, and his lips moved as though he were talking to himself.

"My brother?" he presently asked.

"Yes: he is alive."

But the old man merely shook his head and said nothing.

Graham entertained but one theory regarding the removal of the treasure from Lone Tree—the theory that Covill had advanced—that a priest had betrayed the secret of the confessional, and had taken the money. Having failed to arouse in old Webster's mind any thought of his brother, Graham resorted to an expedient for learning of the priest.

But how should he proceed? The task was the most dangerous and delicate that he had undertaken, as even a bare reference to the subject might unnerve the old man, and render him incapable of making further revelations. Furthermore, Graham had given the old man a larger quantity of whisky than he could bear in his weak condition, and drowsiness was rapidly approaching.

"Are you a Catholic?" asked Graham.

The old man simply stared at him, and made no reply.

Graham decided to come to the point at once, as time was precious.

"Did you confess to a priest that you buried the money under Lone Tree?"

The question had a magical effect. The old man's eyes brightened at once.

"Lone Tree!" he exclaimed.

"Yes; Lone Tree, with the iron pot buried under it."

"Filled with gold—bright, yellow gold—twenty-two thousand dollars in gold!" he gasped. His excitement was intense.

"Where is the money?" asked Graham, pressing the old man hard.

"The money?"

"Yes."

"Lone Tree?"

"Yes."

"Twenty-two thousand dollars. Ah!" and he rubbed his hands and smacked his lips.

Graham laid his hand firmly on old Webster's shoulder, and again demanded:

"Where is the money?"

"The twenty-two thousand dollars?"

"Yes."

"Lone Tree?"

"Yes."

"Buried eighteen years."

This was all the answer the old man could make. Nevertheless, it was apparent that a great struggle was going on in his feeble mind, but the temporary light was fast fading. His eyes rolled in their sockets, and with an effort that was almost ludicrous he shrugged his shoulders and assumed an air of profound mystery.

"Lone Tree?" he asked interrogatively, looking Graham steadily in the face.

"Yes."

"They will all be turned out to-morrow."

So great was Graham's anxiety that it was with difficulty he retained his presence of mind. Still holding his grasp on Webster's shoulder, he gave the old man a shake, and threateningly said:

"If you don't tell where that money is, I'll hang you for murder."

If it was possible for the old man to become paler than he was, his face became as white as that of a corpse; then he again broke down and cried.

"Tell me where the money is," demanded Graham, "and I will let you go."

"The money?"

"Yes."

"Lone Tree?"

"Yes."

"Twenty-two thousand dollars?"

"Yes."

"Iron pot?"

"Yes."

"Buried eighteen years."

This threw Graham into the last stage of exasperation.

With flushed face and with eyes glittering with anger, he dragged the helpless old man to his feet, and violently thrust him against the wall. Then he picked up a carving-knife, and brandishing it in a threatening manner, said:

"Speak, or I'll cut your throat! Where is that money?"

The spectacle that then presented itself was pitiful in the extreme. Old Webster, fully expecting the knife to be thrust into his vitals, closed his eyes, and faintly murmured:

"God, have mercy on me!"

The appeal touched Graham's heart instantly, and he relaxed his grasp, and tenderly seated the old man on the chair.

Some other plan must be adopted. Graham, eyeing Webster narrowly, and endeavoring to impress strongly upon him every word that he uttered, said:

"Listen to me, old man: you wanted to give that money to Graham's son. Well, a priest stole the money, and Graham's son never got it."

"Never got it?"

"No."

"Lone Tree?"

"Yes."

"Twenty-two thousand dollars?"

"Yes."

"My brother stole it."

"Your brother?"

"Yes."
"Henry?"
"Yes."
"Where is he?"
"Eh?"
"Where is Henry?"
"Henry?"
"Yes."
"Lone Tree?"
"Yes."
"Twenty-two thousand dollars?"
"Yes; where is Henry?"
"Henry?"
"Yes."
"Brother?"
"Yes."
"O, he's a rich man."
"A rich man?"
"Eh?"
"Is Henry a rich man?"
"Henry?"
"Yes."
"Lone Tree?"
"Yes. Where is Henry?"
"O, San Francisco."
"What's his name?"
"O, he's a rich man."

In another minute the old man would completely succumb to intoxication. With a violent effort he roused himself, desperately trying to shake off the lethargy that was overpowering him. A moment of half-lucid thought came to his relief, and with it a faint realization of all that he had suffered by persecution. His chest expanded and heaved, and his eyes flashed with anger.

"My brother stole the money!" he shouted. "He knew I wanted to restore it to Graham's boy. He has hounded and hunted me all these years, and wouldn't let me earn an honest living. Ah, the coward! He's a rich man—a very rich man. I'm a poor old beggar. Where's Graham's son?" he asked, looking eagerly around.

"I am Graham's son," answered John.

"Eh?"

"I am Graham's son."

"Graham's son?"

"Yes. What does your brother do? What is his name?"

"My brother?"

"Yes."

"Henry?"

"Yes."

"Lone Tree?"

"Yes."

"Twenty-two thousand dollars?"

"Yes."

"Iron pot?"

"Yes. What is Henry's name?"

"They will all be turned out to-morrow."

The last effort in the struggle against unconsciounsess had

been made, and the collapse had come. The temporary life infused by the liquor had gone. The transitory excitement had passed away, and the weak mind succumbed to intoxication. With a heavy lurch, the old man fell forward upon the floor, and in another moment he was sound asleep.

CHAPTER XVIII.

THE ELEVENTH OF MAY.

THE eleventh of May, in the year of our Lord one thousand eight hundred and eighty—the most remarkable day in the strange history of California, dawned bright and beautiful. When the rising sun peeped over the snow-covered Sierra, it looked down upon an enchanting scene in the valley—upon Visalia, half slumbering in its grand bower of oaks; upon the level plain that lay beyond it to the westward; upon Cross Creek, lined with willows, and bearing its swollen burden to the lake; upon lovely fields of bright young grain that carpeted the whole face of Mussel Slough with a tapestry of tender green; upon tall poplars, standing in stately guard over the less pretentious but more inviting willows; upon the placid lake and the thrifty towns; upon the broad bosom of tree-lined King's River; upon the plains beyond the lake; upon the undulating eastern slope of the Coast Range.

Mussel Slough is more than a garden; it is a hot-house: for no garden could yield such wealth of grain and fruit, such trees of marvelous growth, such busy towns which enlarge with wonderful rapidity. There are three of these towns in the heart of Mussel Slough. Hanford and Lemoore lie some eleven miles north of the lake, and five miles apart, on a line running east and west. Some three or four miles north of nearly the middle point of this line is Grangeville. Hanford and Lemoore are on the line of a branch railroad that taps the juncture of the Central Pacific and the Southern Pacific railroads at Goshen, which is nearly half-way between Hanford on the west and Visalia on the east. This branch road terminates at Huron, a small station a few miles west of Lemoore. Hanford is the largest and most important of the three towns. It has great warehouses for grain raised in Mussel Slough, and broad streets lined with large houses of brick and smaller houses of wood. It is new, fresh, and clean. Its suburbs are strewn with bright cottages, painted white, and provided with green window blinds, and many with dainty flower gardens in front. It is thus with the other towns; and on this memorable eleventh of May there was on all an impressive aspect of prosperity and contentment.

There had been a favorable season, and the grain was unusually luxuriant. Even the more modest alfalfa claimed its share of attention, and had a deeper and richer green than ever before, and added its quota to the beauty of the scene.

And yet it was only a few years ago that this vast garden was a desert wilderness, scoured by bands of cattle, horses, and hogs; and the land was of little value to any one. Every stalk of the bright green wheat that grew there on the eleventh of May; every tender spray of alfalfa; every fruit tree, loaded with its perfumed burden of flowers; every thrifty home and happy household—everything of life, where death had been before—was a monument and a breathing witness to the struggles, hardships, and dire sufferings of those pioneers in Mussel Slough who dug the ditches that carried water into the desert, transforming it into a garden whose loveliness is not surpassed on all the broad face of the earth; dug the ditches in poverty, hunger, and rags, while rich men jibed them and men less brave derided them; dug the ditches to make a home and shelter for their wives and children, who had not enough to eat; worked through burning heat and freezing cold, through water and through choking dust, with the mocking world at their backs and the hope of a peaceful future before them.

They performed prodigious feats of labor, digging miles and miles of broad, deep ditches, that brought down the liquid treasure from the mountain streams.

Let it be remembered, that of the almost countless thousands of acres of land owned by the railroad company, the settlers in those days of hardships had only a few—a patch here and there in the desert. The open, sandy soil drank the water on all sides from the ditches; so that all the country, as well as the small tracts taken here and there by the settlers, was in due time rendered wonderfully productive. The peculiar nature of the soil permitted the water to be carried from the various ditches by percolation throughout all the Mussel Slough country. The land that was heretofore utterly valueless—land held by the railroad company—became so productive, and the demand for it became so great, that the enhanced value consequent upon the toil of the early settlers would have been sufficient to make one man fabulously rich. In all justice, honesty, and decency; in the light of a knowledge of that ground-work of fair dealing on which the safety and the peace of society are founded; in the name of common humanity, and that which is due from one man to another—would not an upright mind have suggested that these first settlers be given the small tracts of land they occupied, upon payment by them of prices agreed upon between them and the railroad claimants before these great improvements were made? This a question for honest men to answer and for brave men to act upon. The eleventh of May stands as the answer of the railroad company backed by the law. The nature of that reply will soon appear.

Let us understand the causes that led to this bloody day. The settlers did not recognize as valid the claim of the railroad company to the lands, believing that the patents from the Government had been issued on false representations; that the road had not been constructed through those parts of the State designated in the articles of incorporation, which articles were the legal basis of the appropriation of lands by the Congress; that the terms of even the appropriation had been violated in three ways: by a failure to make the railroad through Mussel Slough a continuous highway through the State; and by a further failure to construct the entire section of twenty-five miles through Mussel Slough before the land could be legally patented; and by a still further failure to construct in the required time even the twenty miles that were laid. Upon this basis the settlers contested the legality of the patent issued to the railroad company, and laid before the courts their claims as actual settlers. The question had first been opened by the officers of the Government themselves, and this it was that had called the attention of the settlers to the matter. This controversy was one purely of law, and not of feeling. It was founded on the desire of honest and poor men to secure their rights under the law, and carried with it the common rights of all poor men as against the grasping policy of the rich. The railroad company, in accordance with its policy, set about to carry its point by whatever means were available. It was this policy that caused the blood to flow that was spilled on the eleventh of May.

A mere glance is all that can be given at some important features of this history. The settlers had organized themselves into what they termed a "Settlers' League," the principle object of which was that the settlers should share in just proportion among themselves the expenses of pending litigation ; and here let it be published for the first time to the world, that if the secret records of that league could be found, there might be seen running entirely through them, written in a plain hand and with black ink, an explicit understanding and pledge, formulated in more shapes than one, to respect the law, to cheerfully abide by its decisions, and to raise not so much as a finger against its operation; for it was to law and justice that these down-trodden men looked for relief. And not only was it written in the record, but it was the determination of clear-headed and law-abiding men.

They had faith in their cause, believing that right was on their side.

Acting upon the expressed promise made by the railroad company, in printed circulars, that the settlers would not be required to pay the additional value that their improvements gave the lands, the settlers had cause to feel safe, even if so improbable a thing as a decision against them should be rendered by the courts.

An understanding, recent, explicit, well understood, and binding among honorable men, had been entered into between the settlers and the railroad company, that the latter would not bring against the settlers suits for eviction until the then pending questions of legal ownership and of equitable values should be determined. On the 12th of September, 1878, the settlers were astounded at receiving from the railroad company notifications in which the full value of the land was demanded, after all the improvements had been made—a price many times in excess of that asked in the original proposition. It was then that the confidence of the people was shaken. They refused to pay the price.

There was to be a great meeting at Hanford that day. The opinion of an able jurist concerning the status of the land troubles was to be read, and the people made it a holiday. Families left their homes, and flocked into the town by hundreds. It was an occasion for pleasure and rejoicing; for it was understood that the opinion was favorable to the settlers. The men and women wore their holiday clothes, and brought their lunches in ample baskets. Even at an early hour the roads were thronged with merry parties, laughing and chatting as they went to Hanford. Grangeville and Lemoore were depopulated, and farm-houses left without occupants.

The bright warm light that the sun poured down from over the Sierra, the boundless fields of young grain that waved in the passing breeze, causing it to show alternately lighter and darker shades of green, the few late wild-flowers that lined the roads on either side, the birds that chattered in the willows—all contributed to the glory of the day, a day of enchanting loveliness.

Graham arrived early at Hanford. It might have been seen at once that some great anxiety weighed heavily upon him. And good cause there was. He had slept little the night before, for the old man's incoherent words troubled him sorely. He had learned two important things from Webster: that Webster's brother was alive and a rich man in San Francisco, and that "they will all be turned out to-morrow." Who will be turned out? Graham could not rid himself of the idea that the people of Mussel Slough were threatened with a dire calamity; but unwilling to trust his own judgment, he went early the next morning to Hanford, and there sought his friend Newton. He told Newton what the old man had said.

"Impossible!" exclaimed Newton. Then he reflected a moment, and said: "I was told before I saw you that the United States Marshal slept here last night, and that he and two or three other men left early this morning in buggies; but nobody knew where they were going."

Graham and Newton left Hanford to see the marshal, and endeavor to make with him some arrangement that would not render immediate eviction necessary.

It was a pleasant reunion of friends at Hanford—a meeting of neighbors who were bound to one another by stronger ties than ordinary friendship. Nevertheless, there came upon this vast concourse of people, by imperceptible degrees, a feeling of uneasiness. The news concerning the Marshal slowly but surely found its way to all, and brought with it an indescribable feeling of gloom and depression. Sturdy young men became less attentive to the rosy-cheeked girls; a slight shade of pallor crossed the face of many a mother; and men of mature years gathered in little groups apart from the women, and asked one another:

"What does it mean?"

Some said it meant eviction.

"Surely," exclaimed others, "they would not violate their promise to let us alone until our cases are decided!"

There is something grand in a man who refuses to believe ill of his neighbor.

About ten o'clock a man mounted on a horse dashed into Hanford at a furious pace. He was pale with excitement, and his horse was covered with foam.

"Great God, men!" he shouted, as he reined in his horse and crowds flocked around him.

"What is the matter?" cried a hundred voices.

"On Storer's ranch they are butchering the settlers like hogs!"

That great throng of men and women staggered and

gasped. Some had not heard the news, but it flew from mouth to mouth with wonderful rapidity, and became greatly exaggerated, many crying out in despair that a hundred men had been killed.

It would require a stronger pen than this to convey even a faint idea of the remarkable scene that then transpired. Every man, woman, and child felt that the bloody hand of this terrible eleventh of May had seized him by the throat, and sought to strangle him with that fierce strength that brooks no opposition, and that cares as little for the life of a human being as does the mad hurricane for the reed that stands in its way.

After the first shock of depression, came a terrible reaction. Persons rushed hither and thither in wild dismay, and brave men stared at one another in helpless consternation. The despairing screams of women rent the air— women who learned from the messenger that their husbands lay dead upon the field, with their brains blown out. Oh, the frightful anguish of that moment! Oh, the hearts that were broken, and the children that were rendered fatherless!

With breathless haste, and with fingers trembling with fear, and with sinking hearts, and in dire dread of learning the names of others who possibly had been sacrificed, the people hurriedly secured their teams and pushed on to the scene of the tragedy.

CHAPTER XIX.

THE BAPTISM OF BLOOD.

EAVING Hanford, Graham and Newton rode away in the direction the Marshal and the three men with him had taken. As they went, they met many persons going to Hanford.

"Have you seen the Marshal and his party?" Newton asked some of them.

"The Marshal? Is he here?"

This was depressing news, but it had been expected for some time, and his mission was known at once.

"He is on the road," replied Newton, "and we are going to see what he will do. Of course he will eject some settlers."

Some of the men they thus met joined them and turned about.

"I heard something just as I was leaving town," said Graham, "that does not sound encouraging."

"What is that?" eagerly asked Newton.

"That the two men who drove to Hanford this morning, and went out with the Marshal and the land grader for the railroad company, had two shotguns and a rifle in their buggy, and that each had a pair of revolvers."

"What is that for?" asked one of the party.

"I don't know."

Newton looked downcast.

"Surely," he said, "they don't expect a fight. Why, we are unarmed, and we never thought of a fight."

"No," said one; "there mustn't be anything of the kind."

Thus they rode along, increasing their pace; for an indefinable dread took possession of them. One man, who was incredulous, said:

"Why, the railroad company promised us only the other day that it would not prosecute any ejectment suits until our cases should be decided. How can it do such a thing?"

Newton smiled with some bitterness.

"I am not surprised at what has happened," he said.

They had gone four or five miles when they were joined by a man who was considerably excited.

"What has happened?" asked Newton.

"They have thrown Braden's goods into the road," replied the man. "And that isn't all: they left four loaded cartridges on the door-sill."

This was indeed discouraging news.

"Did Braden make any objection?" asked Graham.

"He expostulated with them; but the Marshal told him that, although it was an unpleasant duty, it had to be done."

"What do those cartridges mean?" asked Graham of the man.

"I don't know. Perhaps they were put there as a warning to the settlers of what they may expect if they offer any resistance."

"But we don't want to fight!" exclaimed Newton, with some impatience. "We want merely to see if this thing can't be delayed. Why, it would be a terrible thing to turn us out now, after we have done all the work and spent all the money that is required until harvest. What in the world will become us? We must reason with the Marshal. They say he is a good man; and I think we can get him to defer the service of these writs of ejectment until after harvest, or until our cases have been decided."

The eviction was the sole topic of conversation. The men discussed it from every point of view, and felt dispirited and crushed.

By this time the number of settlers had increased to fifteen, and it was learned that the Marshal and his party had gone northward after dispossessing Braden. The fifteen men were not far behind the Marshal, as they learned from persons they met on the road. A feeling of gloom depressed them, and they rode in silence. Soon they arrived at a turn in the road, and looking before them, across the field that intervened, they saw the Marshal and the three men who were with him. These had just emerged into the field from the yard surrounding the farm-house belonging to Storer and Brewer.

"There they are," said Graham.

Instead of following the turn in the road to the eastward, the settlers removed a panel of the fence, and rode straight across the field toward the Marshal. That officer sat in one buggy with the railroad land grader, and the other was occupied by the two men who were to be placed in possession of the land from which the Marshal was evicting the settlers, and who had bought the land from the railroad company.

Seeing them coming, the Marshal advanced on foot toward them, and met them about sixty yards from where the buggies were. A short parley ensued, in which the settlers endeavored to make some arrangement with the Marshal, whereby the service of the writs of ejectment might be delayed. The meeting was a friendly one, and the Marshal deplored the unfortunate position in which he was placed.

"It is an unpleasant duty," he said, "but I have to do it."

Some of the men were becoming excited; and as an outbreak seemed possible, on account of the exasperation to which the settlers were driven at seeing themselves betrayed, a guard was placed over the Marshal.

While this was transpiring, two or three settlers rode toward the three men who still sat in the buggies, and they were somewhat more than half-way, when a terrible thing occurred. The sight made Graham's heart stand still.

One of the men in the buggy, seeing the settlers approach near, reached for a gun that leaned against the seat, when the other said:

"Don't shoot yet: it isn't time."

A moment afterward a shot was fired, and one of the advancing settlers fell from his horse, with twelve buckshot in his breast.

The battle had opened. Shot followed shot in rapid succession between the settlers and the two men who occupied the buggy in which were the guns.

Graham and Newton stood apart from the others, and

saw this sickening spectacle: saw man set against man, and neighbor against neighbor, and dragged into the jaws of death by that far-reaching thing that saw fit on this occasion to masquerade in the sacred vestments of the law: saw brave men slaughter one another as though heaven instead of hell had brought them to such bloody work.

It was a terrible sight! One of the men in the wagon received a pistol-ball in the abdomen. The other sprung to the ground; and with a shotgun in one hand and a revolver in the other, boldly advanced upon one of the two men who were guarding the Marshal. Between this guard and the advancing man an old feud existed. The guard, seeing the fate that awaited him, endeavored to get behind his horse, which he was holding. The pursuing man went around, and sent a bullet full into the breast of the guard. The wounded man dropped to his knees, clasped his breast, and exclaimed:

"My God! I'm shot!"

Then he staggered to his feet, and received another bullet in the breast. He reeled away, mortally wounded, in the direction of a pool of water. This man was unarmed; and it may here be said that of the fifteen men only seven had pistols, and they were nearly all inefficient weapons.

As this man staggered to his feet and started for the pool, the other guard, who carried a small revolver which was so inferior that the thumb was required to revolve the chamber, advanced and opened fire on the assailant. He emptied his pistol, but none of the shots took effect. The other man fired twice, missing both times. The third shot made a hole in the guard's breast. He staggered backward three or four steps, stopped, straightened himself, and then fell backward.

The scene was becoming more exciting. Riderless horses dashed about.

"For God's sake, bring me my rifle!" cried the man who had finished the two guards, addressing his companion. This man, suffering from a terrible wound, had descended from the buggy, and was lying on the ground. Besides, the horses, becoming frightened, had run away with the buggy containing the rifle.

The frightful details of that affair are apart from the requirements of this tale. Let it be hoped that at some time they will be written by an abler pen than the one which indites this simple tale. Suffice it to say, that as Graham sat there on his horse, he saw a rapid hurrying of men hither and thither; shouts of the excited, and groans of the wounded and dying; a rapid and deadly discharge of firearms; and then all was still.

The fight had lasted but a moment—perhaps less than three minutes—but it seemed an age. One of the men who had come to be placed in possession of the settler's land by the marshal lay writhing in agony, with a bullet in his vitals. The other, a bold, fearless man, was walking away. He walked down the road, turned out into a field, and two hours later he was found lying on his face, a blackened corpse.

It was immediately after the fight that the messenger started for Hanford with the news that changed the holiday into a day of mourning.

Men and women drove rapidly to the spot; and when

they arrived, an awful scene greeted them. Three settlers lay dead upon the porch of the farm-house; and one of the two men who had been in the wagon lay alongside them, in the throes of death. Two wounded settlers lay inside the house. They afterward died. So strange was the fatality of that day, that another settler, who had received merely a scalp wound, and who walked about all day, afterward died from the injury.

No man who was wounded came out of it alive; and eight brave men were slaughtered that day. All of these were married but two; and when their wives and children arrived, the cries of anguish that went up to heaven might have melted to pity even the hearts of stone that had permitted such a scene to be possible. Women fell upon the prostrate forms of their husbands, and begged them to speak but a single word. Little children, brightly arrayed in holiday attire, fondled the cold hands, and wondered at it all.

One by one the bodies were taken away; and toward evening a storm of wind arose, and howled and groaned, tearing over the plains as though the very elements were outraged and driven to furious anger; and then, adding to its groans the cries of the widow and the orphan, it passed furiously on, howling with rage and screaming in agony— on it madly flew, passing over the lake, and lashing its broad bosom, and then on and on, over the plains, over the fields, over the mountains and far away, until it was lost in the night.

The eleventh of May has passed into the history of California. The widows and the orphans that then were made are the fittest monument to commemorate that day. As the years roll by, crowding one upon another until they seem small in the perspective, the eleventh of May will yet stand out alone and ever conspicuous, broad and bloody, raising its red hand in suppliance to the throne in heaven.

CHAPTER XX.

A DISCOVERY.

NEW troubles now assailed Graham. He soon discovered that his visit to the scene of the tragedy had drawn him into complications that might result in the overthrow of his cherished plans. The law, or, more strictly, the power behind the law, felt itself outraged in its mad ride over human rights, and looked around for victims. It made little difference that men who were in no way involved in the catastrophe were selected to receive chastisement.

It is true that the tragedy of the eleventh of May was a terrible calamity to the settlers of Mussel Slough; but they constituted a very small fraction of the people at large. It was not they alone whose vitals had received the thrust that the power of money sent home, but the dearest rights of the people had been assailed. Still it was necessary to complete the work that had been begun; and to that end, suitable men were found who would serve as examples in the undertaking of terrorizing men who believed that the rich and the poor had equal rights before God and man.

Warrants were issued for the arrest of men charged with

the crime of resisting a United States officer in the discharge of his duties. What a grim pleasantry was that! How penetrating the fine sarcasm of it!

When the settlers learned that warrants for their arrest had been issued, those on whom the writs had not been served before general knowledge of the fact was had voluntarily surrendered themselves to the United States authorities at San Francisco, cheerfully paying from their own pockets the expenses of that long journey.

However, there was one exception, and he was Graham. It is true that very few of the men believed that this grim joke perpetrated by the law would be received by a jury as done in earnest; but Graham, for whom also a warrant had been issued, had now one overshadowing duty to perform; and not wishing to delay it by the tedious time he knew would be consumed in the trial, he decided to discharge that duty first, and then to surrender himself. This was to discover Nellie and restore her to her home. The search for the Lone Tree treasure was secondary to that.

Graham was as innocent of participation in that tragedy as he would have been were he a thousand miles away; but that made little difference: for others that were arrested were as innocent as he. He believed he could establish that fact at the trial; but a great uneasiness pursued him on Nellie's account. He would first find Nellie, and then he would surrender himself.

Several days had elapsed before he learned of the issuance of the warrant; and on becoming aware of the fact, he lost no time in proceeding on the mission that had now become the most important of his life.

He had not heard from Covill in a long time, and as yet he did not suspect the treachery of which Covill was guilty. He did not dream that Covill had attempted to take the life of old James Webster, or he would have lost no time in calling the detective to account. Strange as it may seem— and yet it but showed Graham's true nature—he was now the friend and champion of the helpless old man who committed the murder twenty years ago. The atonement that Webster had made fully satisfied Graham so far as the old man was concerned, and the imbecile's sorrows and his helpless condition appealed strongly to Graham's heart.

But where was Webster? He disappeared on the morning of the tragedy in Mussel Slough, and Graham's most earnest endeavors to find him had proved futile. This was a discouraging misfortune, as Graham was still in the dark as to the whereabouts of the treasure. But he was convinced that Covill's theory of the betrayed confessional was wrong— never, however, suspecting that Covill had a bad design in formulating that theory. Graham was convinced that James Webster's brother, learning by some means that James was endeavoring to restore the treasure to its rightful owner, removed it from its resting place under Lone Tree. Next to finding Nellie came the importance of discovering Henry Webster. Graham had already searched a directory to San Francisco, but he could not find that name. It was clear, then, that Henry Webster was living under an assumed name. Indeed, Graham already was morally certain from the outset that both the men had changed their names.

As soon as possible after the occurrence of the tragedy in Mussel Slough, Graham wrote to Covill, informing him of all that James Webster had said, and adding a carefully prepared description of Henry Webster, as he was twenty years before.

Mr. Foster had gone to San Francisco to seek Nellie, but Graham had heard nothing from it. It was only the hope that Foster would make some discovery that prevented Graham's departure on the same mission immediately after the tragedy. But another obstacle had detained Graham: Nellie had, of her own free will, chosen between him and her friends at San Francisco; and John was proud and sensitive. He was not yet prepared to make overtures to Nellie for a reconciliation; and his pride had held him in check. Still, if misfortune had befallen her, John would be the first to show himself a friend in need. There was not the least desire in his heart to see Nellie humbled and brought back to him as a last resort. Indeed, he knew well enough that Nellie's spirit was too proud for such humiliation as that to bring her back to her old friends on the plains. He knew that rather would she cast herself into the bay than return to her home after being cast out by her rich friends. It was such thorough knowledge of her nature that made John all the more uneasy; and it was the possible danger in which her disposition placed her that caused his anxiety to find and rescue her.

"Grandmother," he said one day, "I am going away. I shall be back in a few days."

He did not tell her whither he was going, and she did

not know that a warrant for his arrest had been issued. He thought it better not to inform her.

He mounted his horse and started across the plains; and in due time he arrived at San Francisco. His thoughts had been very busy. He decided that he would exercise great care in preventing a knowledge of his whereabouts being learned by those who sought to arrest him. Nothing was farther from his mind than a desire to avoid the consequences of his presence at the Mussel Slough tragedy, although he took no part in that affair. In good time he would surrender himself, but not until he should discover Nellie.

How could Nellie be found? Without delay John sought the chief of police. That gentleman was not in his office; but as Graham was leaving he met a familiar face. The man looked straight at him, as though endeavoring to remember where he had seen him.

"If I am not mistaken," said Graham, "you are the detective who visited me some time ago, when I was looking for a man to hunt up a case."

"Ah, I remember! By the way," said the detective, "something occurred that day that I was never able to understand."

"What is that?"

"Well, if I remember correctly, you applied to the chief for a detective."

"Yes; and he sent me one."

"He did, and I am the man; but you had employed another."

"Didn't the chief send the other man?"

"No."

"Indeed!"

"I am the only man he sent to you. I spoke to the chief about it afterward, and he came to the conclusion that you had picked up some man. I was half inclined to go to you and warn you against picking up any stranger who came along; but you had acted as if you knew your own business, and certainly it wasn't any affair of mine. What man did you get, anyhow?"

"A man named Covill."

"What?"

"Covill."

"Covill—Covill—let me see; I am pretty sure he is the fellow that works for the railroad company. It is very strange that he should be permitted to take an outside case —a very unusual thing. Well, what business are you on now?"

Graham explained his mission.

"I think she must be all right," said the detective, "as no floaters answering to her description have been picked up. The tide generally brings 'em in, you know—that is, what's left of 'em after the crabs get through. Her uncle has been here several days, but he left yesterday. He asked me to look out for the girl, but as yet I haven't found any trace of her."

Graham walked away in a very thoughtful mood. The information that Covill was a detective for the railroad company was perplexing, and he understood the matter no better than did the detective. He knew not which way to turn. If the detective had failed in securing any information from Mrs. Harriott, how could he hope to succeed?

The following afternoon his attention was attracted by a singular figure he saw on the street. It was that of an old man, slowly hobbling along on a crutch (for he had but one leg). In a moment Graham recognized James Webster, one of the murderers of his father. Graham's heart bounded with excitement. What strange fatality led that old man again across his path?

His first impulse was to overtake and hail the old man; but then he feared that such an unexpected meeting might again render the cripple helpless. With great difficulty restraining his impatience, he followed the old man as the latter carefully picked his way along the street, stopping now and then to glance over his shoulder, seeming to fear that he was followed. Graham pretended indifference, but kept a close watch on the old man's movements. Webster proceeded laboriously; and finally he arrived at a stairway and halted. He read the signs at the door, and then he commenced to climb, slowly and painfully.

He had gone but a few steps when he paused to rest, for the climbing was a difficult undertaking for the feeble old man. He turned his face toward the street, and Graham saw that a somewhat stronger light of intelligence shone in his face than there did when Graham last saw him.

After resting a moment, the old man proceeded. He arrived at the first floor, and then looked around for a certain door. Having found it, he entered without ceremony, throwing the door wide open, so that Graham could see all that occurred within.

A dignified, gray-haired man sat at a table, and he looked up to see the intruder. For a moment he did not seem to recognize the strange man who stared at him; but his memory was soon refreshed.

"I've found you, Henry," said old Webster.

The voice was enough. The gray-haired man at the table started, and then became deathly pale, and then muttered a curse.

"What do you want?" he demanded, vainly endeavoring to regain his self-possession.

"Twenty-two thousand dollars," said old Webster, in a half-idiotic, half-insolent tone.

"Get out, now, or I'll have you arrested," said the other man, sternly.

At that moment Covill entered from an adjoining room. He and old Webster saw each other at the same moment. Covill staggered backward, as if he beheld an apparition from the other world. His pallor and fright were distressing. At the same instant, old Webster, recognizing the man who had attempted his life, threw up his hands, and exclaimed:

"God save me!"

It was a strange and painful scene. The old man, who, having dropped his crutch, leaned against the table for support, stared pitifully at one of the men and then at the other.

A curious problem had presented itself to Graham's

mind, called up by the remarkable scene on which he looked. Without hesitation, he stepped boldly into the room; and without saying a word, he took the old man by the arm, and seated him on a chair.

"Covill," he then demanded, "what does this mean?"

CHAPTER XXI.

A VERY LONG JOURNEY.

NELLIE'S uncle had returned from San Francisco without tidings of the missing girl, and her friends there had treated Mr. Foster with lofty disdain, pretending to know nothing of Nellie's whereabouts, nor the causes that led to her disappearance. Mr. Foster, having no means with which to further prosecute the search, and being a weak and undecided man, had left the matter in the hands of the local authorities.

"I shall be back in a few days," John had told his grandmother when he left, and the hope of seeing him soon again sustained her; but one day she learned that she was to be ejected from her home. Where was her grandson? She did not know. It was then that she felt more than ever the need of his assistance. But time was pressing, and something must be done.

The good old woman resolved to do a noble thing. Without telling any one her intention, she quietly gathered together what money she could, and then suddenly disappeared.

An idler at San Francisco might have seen, if he had

noticed, a feeble, tottering old woman, covered with dust from a long journey, and nearly falling with weakness at every step, slowly picking her way along the noisy streets. The idler might have seen at a glance that she was frightened and shy, and not in the least accustomed to the bustling crowds that hurried past her, scarce noticing her feebleness and confusion. He might have seen her timidly inquiring the way to a certain rich man's house, and continually going astray from the directions that were kindly though roughly given her. He might have noticed the infinite pains that she took to follow the directions closely, and the repeated failures that she made, and the many apologies that she offered for troubling people so often.

But at last her old heart bounded with joy as she found herself ascending the broad stone stairs that led to the door—so feeble and weary with long walking and hunger that the climbing was hard work for her: so hard, indeed, that she was forced to crawl on her hands and knees.

A lackey answered her timid summons; and when he saw the dusty, decrepit old woman at the door, he brusquely demanded:

"Why didn't you go around to the kitchen?"

"I didn't think of that, sir," she said humbly.

"Well, clear out, then!" he commanded, as he was shutting the great door.

"O, but, sir!" she cried, in such agony that his hand was stayed, and he looked at her with considerable curiosity. "O, sir, please tell the master that I want to see him on a very important matter."

"Bah!" ejaculated the servant, as he shut the door with a bang.

The poor old woman sat down and cried like a child; and how long she sat there she did not know; but presently the lackey again appeared, and his indignation and astonishment at seeing the poor old woman at the door were so great that it was with difficulty he repressed a desire to kick her.

"What! you here still?" he demanded.

"I couldn't help it, sir. I couldn't leave without seeing the gentleman."

"Do you want money?"

"Money!" exclaimed the old lady, proudly drawing herself up to her full height. "Money! No; I want to see him about a very important matter."

The servant—not a bad fellow at heart—became interested, and he said:

"If you'll tell me what it is, I'll let him know."

"O, I want so much to speak to him myself. I *must* speak to him. You couldn't make him understand."

"Now, look here, old woman," said the man, "it's no use cutting up like that. You needn't think you can run this house, you know. The boss won't come down unless he wants to. Say your say, and I can tell him what it is; and then if he wants to waste any of his valuable time on you, why, it's none of *my* lookout, you know."

"Well, then, tell him," said the old lady, "that I have come to beg for my home. They are going to turn me out"

"What has he to do with that?"

"O, they say that he has a great deal to do with it. You know my grandson bought the place, and it will be *so* hard for us to give it up."

"O, *he* did?"

"Yes, sir."

"Well, I'll tell the boss; but you needn't think it's going to do you any good."

In a short while the servant returned, with a message to the effect that the master was too busy to see her, and that in any event it would be impossible for him to do anything, as the law had taken its course, and interference was simply out of the question. What irony was that!

This crushed out the last hope that the timid, feeble old woman had. She picked her way down the broad stairs, hardly knowing whither she went, so benumbed with grief was she. She tottered down the sidewalk. Then she could not keep her wits about her very well. After a long time she found herself on a railroad train; and then she remembered that some men had been talking to her, and that one of them had brought her something to eat, and that they asked her a great many questions which she could not understand, and that then they placed her in a carriage, which seemed to roll along the street for days and days, and that soon it halted, and a man helped her out very kindly and gently, and told her not to be afraid, as nobody would hurt her, and that then he assisted her upon the train, and spoke concerning her to a man wearing a cap with a gold band around it, and dark blue clothes trimmed with brass buttons. All these things flitted like shadows through her failing memory, and she half believed that it had all been a dream. And then the dull pain that came upon her at the rich man's house returned, and seemed to be gnawing her heart-strings loose.

Poor, simple old woman! The only brave thing she had ever attempted in all her life to do brought her only bitterness and despair: and it brought more than that, for her mind was shaken.

For hours and hours—and perhaps for days and months and years, for all she knew—the train bore her over the dusty plains—on and on, she thought—always on and on, stopping now and then to take breath for further effort—on and on, puffing and groaning and rattling and grinding—always, and it seemed eternally, carrying her away and away, on the dreary road that leads from time to eternity.

But at last the man with a cap having a gold band came to her and told her he would help her off the train. She thought it was about time; for in a vague sort of way she had been dying all that time—all those hours and perhaps days and months—dying a slow and painless death, and that at last she had reached the haven of rest. And then the dream seemed more real than ever; for when she alighted, she recognized the broad plains and some houses she knew. She felt sure that she was dead, and that her spirit had returned to get John and take him to heaven.

Where was John? She asked that question of a familiar spirit-face that she saw, and the voice that belonged to the spirit—it was such a tender, pitying, manly voice—told her that John had gone far away.

Ah, John! you should not have disappointed her thus. She was sure that you would be there to meet her with your grave smile of welcome, and your strong grasp of her trembling old hand. Ah, John! it was very, very cruel of you to go so far away, and not be there to welcome your old grandmother, who had always loved you with the deepest affection, John.

The kind spirit whom she had addressed offered to take her out in his wagon to her home. At first she thought she could walk the distance, as it was only a few miles away, especially as she was a spirit, and would not be fatigued by the walk; but perhaps her spirit was old and feeble, as well as the body she had left at the rich man's door; for her spirit tottered, and could not walk a dozen steps. But the other spirit—the one with the kind, manly voice, and whom she had known when she was alive—picked her up with perfect ease—for she was merely a spirit, weighing nothing—and placed her in the wagon, and drove away.

It was a sweet and restful ride for a spirit to take. There was very little noise and very little dust, and spirits were not continually coming and going, and slamming doors. It is true that the sun was hot and the plains were barren; but for all that they were very beautiful, for everything is beautiful to a spirit. Sometimes she tried to speak, although she knew that spirits could not talk in in audible voice; and when she did, her voice sounded to her as if it were a long, long way off, and talking from the body that she had left behind. And then she would not talk again, because it was wrong for a spirit to put a voice into the body that it had left.

The spirit in whose wagon her spirit rode told her that he would take her on to his house, but she said she wanted to go home, as John might be there, and he would want to see her. It was a kind spirit that talked to her and tried to cheer her; but although she tried hard to be cheerful, she failed, and could only cry a little now and then.

Soon they came to her house. A great change had taken place there. She saw all her household goods in the road, where they had been recently put. And they were all covered with dust. In particular, one famous quilt, which she had made with her own hands, a great, great many years ago, and which she had treasured from year to year—a many-colored quilt of the finest silk—lay all in a shapeless bundle in the dirt. If she had not been a spirit she would have felt aggrieved at this; but of what use were all those cherished things now?

The spirit with whom she rode begged her not to get out, telling her that her house had been taken from her in her absence, as were those other homes on the day when they had that great fight; but she did not think that any one could rob a poor old woman of her home; and she begged so piteously that he tenderly lifted her from the wagon.

She hobbled to the door, and there she was met by a man whom she had never seen. If John had been there he would have recognized in the intruder the man who discovered him digging for the treasure at the foot of Lone Tree.

"Oh!" he said, in his whining, nasal voice, "you're the old 'un thet was a-holding this place, ain't yer? Well, I guess you'll have to clear out and take yer duds with yer, as the rightful owners of this here house has throwed yer things out and placed me in possession."

"That's an infernal shame!" growled the man in the wagon.

"Well, what could a feller do? Yer see, I wanted a place, and I've got as much right to a home as any of yer; and I paid 'em ther price for this place. The old 'un here wouldn't have a place that doesn't belong to her, would she?"

"I'm not complaining," meekly said the old lady. "I haven't any use for a house now; but I thought maybe John was in there."

"Ha! ha! There's no John in here, I can tell yer, old critter. Yer'll have to go somewhere else if yer want to see yer John. Likely as not he'll be in prison soon."

The man in the wagon jumped to the ground, and grasped his whip in such a manner that the stock could be used to dangerous advantage, and then threateningly advanced on the man in the door. But that discreet person suddenly closed the door and securely bolted it on the inside, while the old lady's angry champion hurled these insults at him:

"You low-lived coward! You *would* stand in with them robbers to drive a poor old woman out on the plains, when her mind is already shaken with trouble!" And then he turned toward Mrs. Graham just in time to see her fall unconscious to the ground. He raised her head, and anxiously spoke to her, but no answer came. She was at the end of her long and dreary journey at last.

"Do you think John will come?" she presently asked in a whisper.

"He will meet you in heaven," said the man, as the tears streamed down his rough but kindly face, and silently fell upon the ground.

Then he placed the gaudy old quilt in the bottom of the wagon, and tenderly picked her up in his great strong arms and laid her thereon.

She smiled sweetly; and then, with the name of John upon her lips, her sweet spirit took its flight to heaven, and the journey was at an end.

CHAPTER XXII.

THE END OF THE SEARCH.

WHEN Graham stepped into the room and confronted the three men, the scene was almost tragic. He had heard old Webster address the white-haired man at the table as "Henry," and the thought flashed across his mind that at last he had found the two brothers face to face.

The shock of meeting Covill proved too great for the old cripple. When Graham seated him upon the chair, he looked up into the young man's face with a piteous appeal for protection; but the light of intelligence that shone in his face while he stood on the stair had faded out, and only helpless imbecility appeared; yet in that look was a pathetic appeal for the help of a friend. He seemed to recognize in Graham such a friend, but it was more an instinct than anything else.

Graham was deeply impressed by the look of indescribable terror with which old Webster regarded Covill; and it was this that caused him to ask:

"Covill, what does this mean?"

It was with the greatest difficulty that Covill recovered

sufficient strength to speak; and even when he did, his face was livid, and he was compelled to support his trembling form by leaning upon the back of a chair:

"What did you ask, Mr. Graham?" he stammered.

At the mention of that name by Covill, the white-haired man who sat at the table suddenly sank, as though a thunderbolt had struck him. The surprise was complete and the result extraordinary. But the man, possessed of remarkable nerve, succeeded so well in partially concealing his emotions, that only Graham noticed the effect his name produced. This removed all doubt from his mind. At last the long hunt for the stolen treasure was at an end, he thought.

But what meant Covill's perturbation? By what mysterious link was he bound to those two men! While gazing intently at the detective, Graham's mind was busily at work. In a moment he resolved upon a course; but for the present he decided not to charge the white-haired man with the crime. He would first work upon the detective.

"Gentlemen," he said, with a respectful air, "you must pardon my intrusion into this room. I happened to pass in time to see this old man come in, and then I discovered you, Covill. I thought I would come in and ask you how our case is getting along."

Covill's heart bounded joyfully.

"Evidently," he thought, "Graham doesn't suspect anything."

With remarkable presence of mind he recovered his self-possession, and hastily said:

"Getting along all right, sir."

"That's good news. I was about to become discouraged."

The white-haired man had also recovered from his surprise; and during these remarks between Covill and Graham he opened a drawer, and quietly looked at a piece of paper. Then he closed the drawer, and with a hand that trembled slightly he wrote a short note, and handed it to Covill. The detective glanced at the direction, and started to leave.

Graham, who had been standing between him and the outer door, quietly said:

"Covill, I want to speak to you before you leave."

"I'll be back in a moment, Mr. Graham. This is an important message concerning some stocks, and has to be attended to at once. I'll be back immediately."

But this smooth speech did not deceive Graham. He did not divine the meaning of the note, but he was determined that no advantage should be taken of him.

It was while he was in this strange situation that he began to feel within him a dangerous uprising of all that was ferocious in his nature. It somewhat alarmed him, as he had never before experienced such a sensation. It was a rising desire to murder these two men on the spot. As yet he had perfect control over himself, but he feared that unless he could keep himself calm and collected, serious consequences would come about; and the strongest factor in this effort at self-control was his love for Nellie and his grandmother.

It was with cool determination and firmness that he quietly said to Covill:

"Wait a while, Covill. My business is too pressing to spare you now."

"But I *must* go," urged Covill, attempting to pass the young man.

"You must *not* go, Covill," said Graham, firmly grasping the lapel of Covill's coat, and unceremoniously seating him upon a chair.

Covill saw danger, and quietly submitted; but the white-haired man, who sat at the farther end of the table, arose to his feet, and with an imperious voice and gesture, said:

"Young man, this is my office, and I am not accustomed to seeing strangers come here and take charge of my affairs in any such way. This man Covill is employed by me, and has no authority to listen to the orders of others. Covill, deliver that note."

Graham, still standing, folded his arms, and looking steadily at the white-haired man, said:

"I know that I may appear officious, but I have important business with this man. I desire that he remain where he is. Not only that, but I shall, with your permission, take a slight precaution against interference."

Almost as soon as he had ceased speaking he had locked the two doors, and placed the keys in his pocket.

The white-haired man knew little of the character of Graham, or he never would have pursued the course that he then adopted. He decided to carry off the scene with bravado.

"This is an outrage!" he exclaimed. "Open those doors, sir, or I shall call a policeman from the window."

"You—had—better—not," said Graham, with the utmost deliberation. "Keep quiet, sir. I would have treated you with some deference if you had acted differently; I have business with you as well as Covill."

"Business with me? I desire to have no business with you, sir."

"Keep quiet; it will be better for you," said Graham, in a low voice; but his face was becoming white, and his fingers opened and closed in an ominous manner.

The white-haired man, seeing that his plan had failed, resumed his seat. He saw that the moment was a critical one, and that a word too much might send him without ceremony to the other world.

Graham then turned his attention to Covill.

"Covill," he said, "give me that note. I can deliver it as I go down the street."

Covill started, and turned pale, and then glanced appealingly at the white-haired man, who was aghast at the daring impudence of Graham's demand.

"Give me that note, Covill," said Graham, his voice becoming louder, and his face changing from pallor to a flush.

As he made this second demand, he strode threateningly toward the cowering detective, as though he would choke him. In order to save himself from violence—for Covill believed that the impetuous young man would stop at nothing—he produced the note, and mincingly extended it toward the furious young man.

Graham took the note, and immediately opened and read it. The note was as follows:

"U. S. Marshal: You have a warrant for Graham. He is at my office. Hurry.   "H."

"Ah!" exclaimed Graham. "That was neatly done, wasn't it, Covill? Why, you needn't be uneasy on that score. I intend to surrender myself in good time."

His manner was more pleasant, but none the less determined. Then it occurred to him that it was an extraordinary thing for the white-haired man to be cognizant of the warrant. A moment's reflection, however, convinced him that it was perfectly natural in the white-haired man to desire Graham's imprisonment, and that he would doubtless keep himself fully informed of all matters that concerned Graham.

"It was very neatly done," Graham repeated; "it's a pity that it failed. Well, as I said, I'll deliver the note very soon. In the mean time, Covill, there are one or two little matters that I want you to explain. You may remember that, as I entered this room a few minutes ago, I discovered you in profound astonishment at seeing this old cripple, and I asked you what it meant. What did it mean, Covill?"

The detective could only stare at Graham in helpless dismay; but presently he said, recovering himself quickly:

"Why, don't you suspect who that old man is?"

"Who is he, Covill?"

"He is the man who murdered your father, and buried his money under Lone Tree."

Catching these words, old Webster, who had been staring vacantly at the three men, straightened himself, and looked around—an old habit when his clouded mind was grappling with some problem.

"Lone Tree?" he asked, looking up into Graham's face.

"Yes," answered Graham.

"Twenty-two thousand dollars?"

"Yes."

"Iron pot?"

"Yes. Do you know this man?" asked Graham, pointing to Covill.

A strange look of horror came into the old man's face as he turned his glance upon Covill.

"Poor old fellow!" hastily interposed Covill. "He's crazy, and evidently thinks I am some one he knows."

"Do you know him?" asked Graham.

Covill's assertion that the old man was insane had a strange effect. Old Webster's eyes flashed with anger and indignation, and he scrambled to his foot and vehemently said:

"They say I'm crazy. I'm not crazy! You want to murder me, do you? Murder me while I sleep!"

Covill sprung to his feet and advanced toward the old man, but Graham's strong arm thrust him back.

"I know the old man's mind is wrong," said Graham; "but that doesn't prevent his telling the truth. Sit down, Covill. If you interrupt him again I'll strangle you!"

The white-haired man, who all this time sat silent at the other end of the table, was placed in an undignified position. Again did he attempt to put an end to the scene.

"This is outrageous!" he exclaimed. "I demand that this farce come to a close."

"Be quiet," calmly said Graham, who, feeling himself master of the situation, was cool and determined. "It seems to me," sternly added Graham, "that you must by this time suspect that some great wrong has been done, and that if you are a man and a gentleman you will do all you can to assist me."

"I am not an officer of the law."

"That's very true; but it would look rather bad if you should appear anxious to let crime escape unpunished."

This ingenious speech had the desired effect, for it led the man to believe that Graham had no suspicions concerning him. Indeed, he decided at once to appear Graham's friend.

"Crime!" he exclaimed, looking from one to the another; "I don't understand. Who has committed a crime?"

Covill, alarmed at this apparent desertion by his friend and fellow-conspirator, hastily protested.

"Why," he said, "this young man is listening to the old imbecile's stories. I don't know of any crime that has been committed."

"Not so fast, Covill," interrupted Graham. "Let us first hear what this old man has to say. Do you know this man?" he asked Webster, pointing again to Covill.

"Yes, yes; I know him. He tried to murder me on the San Joaquin. I was asleep, and—"

"It's all a lie!" shouted Covill.

"Ah, you coward! This is my friend, and he won't let you murder me now."

"What did he want to murder you for?"

"Murder me?"

"Yes."

"Lone Tree?"

"Yes."

"Twenty-two thousand dollars?"

"Yes."

"Ah, the coward! He tried to murder me in my sleep."

"What for?"

"Eh?"

"What did he want to murder you for?"

"Murder me?"

"Yes."

"Lone Tree?"

"Yes."

"I know! I know! Ah, I know! Ha, ha, ha! Tried to murder me, so that I couldn't give the money to Graham's boy."

This was an astounding revelation to Graham.

"Don't say a word, Covill. I don't pay much attention to the old man's stories. Still you must know that I am greatly interested in this matter."

"It's all a lie!" protested Covill. "I never saw him before."

"That is all right, Covill. Don't let that trouble you. Now I want you to pay close attention to a question that I am going to ask you. You received my letter giving you a description of this old man's brother, didn't you?"

"Yes," answered the detective, helpless and crushed.

"Have you that letter with you, Covill?"

"Yes."

"I wish you would read it again."

Covill meekly complied.

"You have never found the original of that description, have you, Covill?"

"No," answered Covill; and this time he was honest.

The heart of the white-haired man beat violently, but by a powerful effort he maintained outward composure.

"It says he had rather a thin face, and his eyes were brown, and he was tall and straight, doesn't it, Covill?"

"Yes."

"And you have never seen such a man?"

"Never."

"About what age ought he to be now, Covill?"

"Between sixty and seventy years."

"Very good. Do you think there is anybody in this room that answers to that description, Covill?"

The detective stared at him in blank amazement.

"Anybody in this room?" he asked, looking quickly around.

"Yes."

"Why, certainly not."

"Look again, Covill."

A broad ray of light suddenly illuminated the darkness of the detective's mind, and with a gasp he sank back in his chair as he recognized the murderer—the white-haired man who sat at the table. It was a genuine surprise, and a terrible one to Covill.

And he was not the only one who sat aghast. Henry

Webster—for the white-haired man indeed was he—could not have received a more terrible shock if a knife had been put between his ribs.

"What do you mean?" he hoarsely demanded, as he sprung to his feet in the wildest excitement.

Graham deliberately walked around the table, and stood before him.

"It means that you are Henry Webster, and that some twenty years ago you and your brother—that helpless old imbecile sitting there—murdered my father in the San Joaquin Valley, and buried his money under Lone Tree. Ah, you didn't know that I was so well informed! But I haven't told you half that I know, you cowardly villain! You were too great a coward to return to Lone Tree and dig up the treasure until you heard that your brother was determined to restore it; and then you disguised yourself in the sacred garments of a priest, and went to Lone Tree and dug up the money, and took it away like a thief. You didn't have one thousandth part of the honesty and manhood of your poor old brother. You were a rich man already, but that didn't satisfy you. You must rob a poor young man and a helpless old woman of what belonged to them by right. O, you never knew how I discovered that shrewd trick of getting yourself killed by the Indians! You never knew that I went down to the bottom of your grave and found your coffin filled with sticks and stones instead of your worthless carcass. O, you may well turn white and tremble! But I haven't yet told all that I know. Your spies were watching me, and they soon informed you that I had come to San

Francisco and applied for a detective. It was then that you sent this miserable fellow to me, to throw me off the track, and beguile me with false theories of betrayed confessionals, and the like. You did it well, Covill, but Heaven and right were against you. You may well sit there and gaze at me in that stupid way; but you needn't think that I have finished. The worst of it all is yet to come. One crime leads to another; and so you were compelled to resort to such an extreme measure. You knew well enough that your brother would learn that Lone Tree had been robbed of its treasure, and that he would know you had committed the robbery, and that he would seek me and tell me all. It was then that you decided upon a desperate plan. You employed this fellow, Covill, to do the bloody work. You hired him to murder your own brother. Don't start and try to gasp some denial. I know it all too well. But see how shrewd you were! You fooled even Covill, who never suspected until this moment that you are the brother of the man he tried to murder. Covill, you ought to be thankful to me for opening up to your gaze such a grand opportunity for blackmailing your worthy employer. Well, Henry Webster, what have you to say for yourself?"

This long speech was made in a burst of inspired eloquence; and those problems that he had not already worked out solved themselves as he spoke. He saw through the plot; and so great was his indignation and rage that his hot words poured out like a stream of molten metal, scorching and burning where it fell. No guilty man could carry a bold face under such terrible denunciation.

15

Henry Webster sat speechless. It seemed that he was choking, for he made an effort to loosen his cravat.

Covill, clearly seeing now what his penetration had not fathomed before, was stunned by the discoveries that Graham had made. With an effort he gained his feet, and with his old sense of cunning, he looked indignantly at Henry Webster, and said loftily:

"Judge Harriott—"

Graham eagerly caught at that name, and interrupted Covill:

"Did you call this man Judge Harriott?"

"Yes: didn't you know he is Judge Harriott?"

"Ah!" exclaimed Graham, as this new revelation burst upon him.

It was a wonderful surprise, and for a moment Graham was powerless with astonishment. With the keen mental penetration that the excitement of the moment invested him with, he at once grasped a solution of the whole mystery.

"I understand it all now," he said. "Webster, you are a far deeper scoundrel than I thought you were. I see through it all now. I know now why Nellie was picked up by your wife. And so, Webster, you are behind all this wonderful plot!"

Graham was silent a moment through wonder, and then he proceeded:

"I see now that you are at the bottom of it all. You thought that Nellie had sufficient influence over me to cause me to accept a position under your patronage, hoping to place me under obligations to you, in order that you might get me in your power. A very shrewd scheme that was, Webster. I suspected it then, but I didn't understand it. When you found that Nellie could do nothing with me you kicked her out into the street. We'll see about that directly. And so it wasn't alone because I was a Mussel Slough settler that you wanted to put a gag into my mouth. You had a private reason, eh, Webster? And that accounts for the warrant for my arrest on a charge of resisting a United States officer. You wanted to get me under lock and key, didn't you, Webster? And it also accounts for that note you gave Covill just now. You wanted me placed under arrest before I could learn anything by seeing your imbecile old brother face to face with you. You are a very, very shrewd man, Webster; and it is a pity to spoil such a nice plot. Now, Webster, let us talk about Nellie. Where is she?"

"I don't know."

A strange change had come over Henry Webster—formerly Judge Harriott. The shock had told upon him. He was in a condition of great nervous prostration.

"Tell me where she is," demanded Graham, becoming furious.

"I don't know."

"I tell you she must be found!" said Graham.

His anxiety on Nellie's account was so great that it outweighed every other consideration. He was willing to lose everything else if Nellie could only be found.

"I am going to make a proposition to you: I will leave

now, and continue my search for Nellie; but I warn you, Webster, and you too, Covill, that if I am arrested before that girl is found, somebody will pay for it. You can put me into jail for a year or two, because the company that you work for knows how to put innocent men into jail; but after a time I shall be free. I shall surrender myself after Nellie is found. You must find her, Covill."

Graham then unlocked the doors and left, taking the helpless old cripple with him. The interview had continued so long that the night was rapidly approaching; and on that account Graham failed to see a slender woman, dressed in black, who followed him and the cripple.

CHAPTER XXIII.

A TREASURE LOST AND A TREASURE FOUND.

AFTER Graham's departure with the cripple, Henry Webster sat a long time in silence—so long, in fact, that the shadows of evening crept into the room, and the light from many lamps on the street below shone through the windows, lighting up the ceiling of the room with ghostly effect. The two men were absorbed in their thoughts. At last the elder man moved uneasily, as though he expected Covill to say something.

"We are ruined," said the detective, gloomily.

There was no reply. Then Covill paced the room, and went around the table in order to be nearer his employer. At last the latter said:

"You are a fool, Covill."

"Sir?"

"You are a fool."

"Well, what is to be done?"

Webster straightened himself in his chair, and said:

"We must put this young man out of the way?"

"How?"

"Listen: he came into this room unbidden; and before I had time to do anything he thrust a pistol in my face and demanded money. You were present, and you dared not move for fear he would shoot you. Do you understand?"

If the darkness had not been so great the elder man might have seen that Covill's eyes sparkled with pleasure.

"None can fail to credit our testimony, and we can send him to the penitentiary."

"Yes; but he will get out sometime."

"There will be time to see about that. Do you know where Graham is staying?"

"Yes, I think I do. In any event, there will be no trouble in finding him."

"Very well. Go immediately to his house and secrete some money there. Then go to the central police station and lodge a complaint against him, charging him with highway robbery. We can afterwards arrange the details of our testimony. Don't fear anything, Covill. It's the simplest matter in the world for a man in my position to get all the testimony we want, and to secure a jury to suit us.'

"All right, sir."

Covill took some money that Webster gave him to secrete in Graham's house, and was about to leave, when he bethought him of another mattter.

"By the way, Judge, can't you let me have some money?"

"How much do you want, Covill?"

"About two thousand dollars."

The other man winced. but he drew a check for that amount.

Before midnight Graham was aroused by a loud knocking at the door. He soon appeared, when a heavy hand was laid on his shoulder.

"I want you," said the intruder.

"What for? Who are you?"

"O, that's all right, you know. I'm an officer; and I want you for that nice little job you worked to-night—highway robbery."

"Highway robbery?"

"Yes."

"Who makes the charge?"

"A man named Covill."

"Ah!"

Graham then understood it all. They desired to get him out of the way.

When he was locked up in a cell he bitterly complained of his fate, and said:

"Is it possible that because a man is poor such things can happen to him? Is the power of money so great that it can but raise a finger, and everything that stands in its way is swept aside?"

His examination was conducted with due pomp, and he was held to answer before a higher court. He was too proud to seek bail; and he believed that so gross an injustice as his conviction could not be done. In his own consciousness he knew that he had not committed the crime with which he was charged. How, then, could he be convicted?

He never learned of his old grandmother's death; but as

soon as he could he wrote her a letter, telling her that he expected soon to arrive, and that he had found the Lone Tree treasure. It was a cheering letter, and if the patient old lady had been alive it would have done her heart good to read it.

His greater anxiety was not for himself, for thoughts of Nellie weighed heavier by far that did his own troubles.

It is unnecessary to describe that trial. Graham was ably defended, but the influence against him was far too strong. At last the sentence came—a year in the State prison at San Quentin. The time that had elapsed since the beginning of the trial was so long that Graham's senses had become blunted. In two days more he would be taken to San Quentin.

During the two days that elapsed, it seemed to him that the life within him was dead. None can picture the agony of such torture as can bring about that result in the breast of a strong, brave, hopeful young man. He asked for his grandmother a hundred times, for he felt that the shock would kill her; but none could give him tidings of her.

A day passed. To-morrow he would be taken to his destination.

About eight o'clock that night, a shabbily-dressed young woman applied at the prison for permission to see Graham. She was pale and emaciated, and several hard lines in her face showed that she had undergone great suffering.

After some demurring, an officer conducted her through a long corridor, and opened a small iron wicket in the door of a cell.

"Here's a visitor, young fellow," he said to the prisoner within.

A haggard face appeared at the wicket, and the trembling voice of the young woman faintly exclaimed:

"John!"

He peered at her through the gloom that pervaded the corridor, at first recognizing neither the voice nor the face; and then a great light broke upon him, and all aghast, he said:

"Nellie!"

There was a tenderness and sorrow in the utterance of that name—a reviving of sweet and sacred memories of the past—that went down into her heart; and she leaned her weary head upon the wicket and burst into tears.

He gently stroked her hair, and with a voice shaken with emotion, he said:

"You have come at last, Nellie! Poor Nellie! Where have you been all this time, my child? and why did you leave us, who loved you so much? Your uncle looked for you so long; and we were very unhappy about you, Nellie! We feared that something serious had happened to you. What has been the trouble, dear Nellie, tell me?"

She wept all the harder for the tenderness that he showed, and said, through her sobs:

"I was ashamed to go back, John."

"Ashamed? Why, Nellie, what could you do to be ashamed of?"

"O, I was so headstrong, and treated you so shamefully, and would not listen to your advice."

"Yes; but that is all forgotten in the great pleasure of seeing you again. Now tell me what has happened to you."

"Spare me, John!"

"Tell me, Nellie," he gently urged.

She sobbed quietly for some time, and then John said again:

"Tell me, Nellie."

"They never had a good purpose in befriending me, John; and when they saw that I could no longer be useful to them, they slighted and snubbed me, and treated me like a servant. O, I understand it all now! I know now that they wanted to make a slave of you, as you said, and that they wanted me to help them. They talked so shamefully about you that I flew at last into a passion, and called them hypocrites and heartless schemers. Then I left them, and refused to take any of the fine things they had given me; and ever since that time I have tried to make a living by sewing. But it is so hard—so hard! And many a time I have gone hungry."

"Poor Nellie! Poor Nellie!" said John, softly, while he continued to stroke her hair; "didn't you know that you would have made us so happy by coming back? You should have come to us, Nellie."

"I couldn't," she exclaimed, in despair. "I couldn't do that, John."

"Well, come now; that will do," said the jailer. "You must go now."

Nellie looked despairingly around, and pleaded:

"O, I have something else to say to him. Please, sir, let me stay a moment longer."

Ah! that humble pleading could not have come from the Nellie of old. Poor, poor Nellie, indeed! Her proud spirit was broken, and humbled to the dust.

"Hurry up, then," said the jailer, gruffly.

Nellie thrust her face as far as she could through the wicket, that the listening jailer might not hear, and blushing so deeply that it could be seen even through the gloom, she hurriedly whispered:

"John, I pity you, oh, so much! I would be willing to lay down my life for you, John."

"Nellie!"

"Don't interrupt me. I have something to say to you. John—"

"Well, Nellie?"

"I don't know how to say it John," she exclaimed, in despair.

"Tell me, Nellie."

"John, do you—do you think, John—that—that you could love me now?"

"Nellie! I love you more than I ever did in my life."

"O, John, it makes me so happy!" and she sobbed afresh, and seized his hand and covered it with kisses. "John, that isn't all I had to say. John—O, how can you love me now, John?"

"Nellie, Nellie! I love you with all my heart."

"Do you think that you would like to have me think of you in—in a very tender, yearning way, while you are in prison?"

"Yes, Nellie; and I hope you will. It will give me strength and hope."

"And do you think, John—do you think that you would—that you would like to have me wait for you—wait for you—as your wife?" and she buried her face in her arm to hide her blushes.

"Nellie," he replied, sadly and thoughtfully, "when I shall be set at liberty, I shall be a ruined man, on whom the most degrading mark of the law has been set, never to be lived down nor worn away. I will be called a convict, and people will shun me, and point me out as a man who is not worthy the esteem of other men. I love you deeply, Nellie; but I love you too much to ask you, when I shall be liberated, to become my wife."

"You don't understand me, John. I didn't mean *then*."

The light that then burst upon him staggered him and rendered him speechless.

"I know, John, that it is a very strange and unwomanly thing for me to do, but I believe it's my duty—and—and I want to be your wife, John! I will write you cheering letters; and when they let you out, you can come to me, and we will be so happy!"

As she spoke, the old brightness that had won John's heart years ago came back to her eyes, which beamed with love and hope.

"Do you mean, Nellie," asked John, hardly able to believe his ears, "that you want us to marry now?"

"To-morrow, John," replied Nellie, still hiding her face.

"But, Nellie, I am a ruined man—ruined now and for all time!"

"Don't say that, John!"

He was silent for some moments, seemingly in hesitation.

"You can't deny me, can you, John? You can't turn me out on the world as those heartless people did!"

His arm stole through the wicket and around her pretty neck, and he impressed a kiss upon her lips.

"It shall be as you say, Nellie. It will give me new hope and life, and it will dispel the desolation that has stretched before me. Perhaps it will be better for us both, dear Nellie."

She raised her smiling face, which was wet with tears, and laughed softly in the sweet old way that was so dear to John, and playfully said:

"Well, good night, my—" and she leaned forward and whispered in his ear—" husband. I'll have to be the man, and get the license and the preacher. That is funny!"

Then she hurried away, and the jailer closed the wicket with a snap and a gruff "Good night."

The next morning there was a quiet wedding in the office of the jail, and Nellie and the convict were made man and wife. Graham's face was brighter and his hope was surer than it had been for many days; and he took with him to prison the bright anticipation that awaited him, when he should regain his liberty and claim his wife.

www.ingramcontent.com/pod-product-compliance
Lightning Source LLC
Chambersburg PA
CBHW031744230426
43669CB00007B/473